Dear Mary,

Best Wishes & Gods'

blessing!

Fr. Roland Maloley, S.J.

NARCO PRIEST

Narco Priest

by Father Roland Melody, S.T.

The World Publishing Company
New York and Cleveland

Published by The World Publishing Company

Published simultaneously in Canada
by Nelson, Foster & Scott Ltd.

First printing—1971

Library of Congress catalog card number: 70-133482

Printed in the United States of America

WORLD PUBLISHING
TIMES MIRROR

To my
parents
and
brothers and sisters

Contents

ACKNOWLEDGMENT

I would like to express my gratitude to all the officers and men of the Narcotics Squad of New York City with whom I had the very special privilege of traveling. I never ceased to be impressed by their dedication and concern for the terrible problem of drug abuse. Their task is a difficult one, and I came to understand more clearly the obstacles and dangers they must face every day in trying to get the job done. I thank them for their many hours of patient explanation and practical street work. The knowledge I gleaned has proved invaluable on numerous occasions, knowledge not always found in textbooks.

I thank them most of all for helping me become a better instrument in the service of others.

Prologue

I am a Roman Catholic priest. On a number of occasions I have worked closely with the Narcotics Squad of the New York Police Force.

I became directly involved in the problem of drug addiction in 1962 when I was invited to speak on narcotics to a group of five hundred parents. Half my allotted time was to be a question-and-answer period. I had read many articles on drug abuse, but I felt my second-hand knowledge would be inadequate. Consequently, I went to the New York City Narcotics Bureau and asked permission to ride with the Narcotics and Undercover Squad whenever I had the opportunity. This, of course, was done at my own risk, and papers were signed to that effect.

Studies tell you that eighty per cent (some even go as high as ninety per cent) of hard-drug users previously used marijuana. True, there is no scientific cause-and-effect relationship between marijuana and harder drugs, but this does not obliterate the danger. I am not dealing in statistics. I am talking about people's lives. If it's possible to become an alcoholic, that possibility should be seriously considered before starting to drink. If it's possible to contract cancer by smoking cigarettes, some sort of warning should be given regarding that possibility. Therefore, and most emphatically, if it's possible to become a strung-out junkie because of marijuana, this ultimate horror of human destruction—drug addiction—should be described in graphic detail.

Narco Priest deals mainly with the first-hand knowledge I acquired while traveling with the Narcotics Squad in New York City—the use and abuse of certain drugs, the type of people caught up in them, and some positive directives in dealing with this very serious and growing problem.

Needless to say, the drug problem is an enormous and complex one. One not to be solved, on the one hand, by the legal extremes of the alarmist or the misinformed, or, on the other hand, by the extremes of those who try to make absolute license a term synonymous with responsible freedom. In this context I feel my book has something to contribute.

Father Roland Melody, S.T.
Stirling, New Jersey
August 1970

1

First Encounter

We had just pulled up to the curb in front of an old brownstone house in Brooklyn. I was in an unmarked car with two detectives from the New York City Narcotics Squad. We were investigating a call that a man living in the building was keeping a girl supplied with narcotics.

Even though the Bureau Chief of Narcotics had tried to prepare me for many of the brutal and dehumanizing scenes I would witness and the dangers I would encounter, even though I had been drilled on police procedure during raids, and even though I was traveling incognito with two of the toughest and best narcotics detectives in the business —I, like the greenest rookie on his first assignment, was just plain scared.

Back of Borough Hall toward the Gowanus Canal the old homes and apartments became progressively more derelict. A bouquet of smells hung in the stagnant air—acetone from the paint factories, a hundred years of dry rot and despair, and last week's uncollected garbage. Rusting skeletons of cannibalized cars vied with greasy, broken sofas for space in the gutters. The car had barely stopped when the pile of rags on a decaying mattress several feet beyond slowly rose and wavered toward us. The agitated scarecrow figure, barely recognizable now as a woman, poked her hand through the open window beside me, jabbing and clawing at the air by my face. The detective in the driver's seat leaned across me and yelled, "Annie, hey there, Annie! How's tricks tonight? Find any live ones?" Startled at hearing her name, she jerked her hand away from the car window, muttering something unintelligible. She had no teeth.

"Some beauty, eh, Father? She's harmless."

"Down here junkies call her kind 'scags!' How old would you guess she is? Sixty? Sixty-five? Seventy? Well, I got curious one time and looked up her record—ten arrests for soliciting and two convictions for possession of heroin. She's an ex-hooker from the World War II days. She's only forty-five."

I was brought up in some pretty scrappy neighborhoods, and I've seen my share of man's inhumanity to man, and the harm people can do to themselves. I've spent time in hospital emergency rooms watching bleeding and broken bodies straining to hold on to an immortal soul. Still, I was moved at the sight of this woman. Maybe because she conveyed so unexpectedly and starkly the possible ultimate horrors of addiction.

There are as many theories about drug addiction as there are professions propounding possible solutions. Psychiatrists tell us to look for significant prepsychotic evidence. Physiologists scrutinize the effects drugs have on the body. Anthropologists report that addiction is all a response to a particular cultural fabric. Statisticians overpower you with figures showing that addiction increases during periods of depression or war, and psychoanalysts note a complex personality deficiency in addicts.

Fine. But on that particular night on that particular

Brooklyn street, all the scientific data seemed so impersonal, so insignificant. Who had helped this poor wretch recently? Who knew she even existed? Had anyone ever reached out to touch this derelict as she blinked in and out of euphoric stupor?

Actually, she was not old. Hard addicts, long-standing mainliners, "cookers" as they are known in their own desperate way of life, do not get a chance to grow old. A forty-five-year-old addict is a Methuselah in the junkie world. They die from all sorts of things indirectly caused by addiction. Complete obsession and preoccupation with drugs, especially heroin, excludes any type of normal eating or sleeping. The natural result of this is severe malnutrition and physical weakness. This eventually makes the body vulnerable to almost anything, with very little resistance once sickness invades. Venereal diseases contracted through prostitution cripple and eventually kill scores of addicts. And prostitution is almost invariably a necessary adjunct to addiction because "turning a trick" is the quickest way to acquire the large sums of money demanded by the drug pushers.

This woman with her blotched skin webbed with veins looked as if she couldn't stand much more. She stood on the brink of physical death, but there was no doubt that her spirit had withered and died long ago. All her natural talents were numbed and mummified. The God-given ability to appreciate things with a healthy mind and body, an ability which is a lifetime adventure of trial and error, talking and listening, hurting and loving, was stunted by the fraudulent promises of chemical crutches. I pressed two quarters into her hand. Just enough to get her some hot soup, more probably cheap wine, but not enough to be able to do herself any further harm with narcotics.

Exposing her decayed gums in what passed for a smile, Annie carefully adjusted a large rusty safety pin on the front of her shapeless housedress as if it were a diamond broach. Then she shambled down the street and was gone. As the three of us got out of the car, the sergeant said softly:

"Father, that's what twenty-five years of mainlining heroin and a few prison terms can do for you. I'm glad you saw her your first time out. She's the most perfect example of the horrors of narcotics addiction I could show you. Too bad we can't bring Annie along when we give narcotics lectures in the schools. One look at her ought to be enough to keep any kid straight!"

The apartment of the man suspected of dealing in drugs was on the first floor. He opened the door as soon as the detectives knocked. I had conjured up in my mind a weasel-type character, a shifty parasite who heartlessly drained his victims. The man I saw standing in the doorway was old, with a mild demeanor and very disheveled. His apartment had a pungent human odor. It was dirty and cluttered. He had succumbed to the frequent evolution that takes place when a man lives alone for too long a time. He had become an inveterate saver and an incorrigible slob.

The man was vague and confused when the detectives began questioning him concerning the girl. In bits and pieces he told us that a girl, Josie, came to his apartment once or twice a week to clean and keep him company. She may have been proficient in the latter; but cleaning was not one of her talents. He admitted that he knew the girl had taken narcotics at one time. But he was not aware that she was still using drugs or that she was a prostitute. He was a retired Navy man and was giving her 150 dollars a month. We learned later she was using every penny of it for drugs. The old man was being taken; he should have known better, but I still felt sorry for him. The detectives warned him to stay away from her, and we left him sitting in his dingy apartment visibly shaken.

The statement that drug addiction is a disease may be a valid one. But certainly its sphere of influence is more terrible than any other disease. No person with cancer or tuberculosis ever inflicted the pain or brought about the destruction and havoc in the lives of others as the addict invariably does. Family, friendships, dignity, and eventually the very fabric of society itself is ruptured by the addict's pitiable and voracious appetite for drugs.

And yet, even in the face of this awful regressive eventuality, the worst action we can take is to try and whip the addict into remorseful penance, hoping to motivate a change. The reaction, "How could you do this to us," is a natural one, but not the best. The addict or potential addict is already a misfit to himself. He cannot believe that people will accept him for the person he is. He feels isolated and inadequate. He can survive only by escaping from the pressures and realities of normal social relationships. And once he discovers, either purposefully or accidentally, that all the love, security, and acceptance he needs can be injected right into his vein, any obstacle to that end, no matter how sacred, must be subverted or eliminated. The old man was probably only one name on a long list of people grimly affected by this girl's unfortunate addiction. The old man had given us the girl's address. Her apartment was only two blocks away on State Street, on the third floor of a four-story tenement.

We went back to the car and drove to the State Street address. Entering the ancient tenement as quietly as possible, we inched up the worn stairs toward the third-floor landing, until our heads were level with the hallway floor. From there we could look under Josie's door and see lights and shadows crossing the threshold. The lights snapped off when she heard us approach. The detectives aligned themselves on either side of the door before knocking, while I remained on the landing. They knocked again and again.

Minutes passed. Suddenly Josie's door opened. She was not alone. Two other girls, both of them younger, stood with her. After a quick look inside, the detectives motioned me in.

As I stepped inside the apartment, the stench of human excrement was overpowering. A set of works lay in full view, ready for use, on the dirty oilcloth top of a makeshift orange-crate table—the only piece of furniture in the front room. Through the open door of the second room I could see two stained mattresses arranged on the floor against the far wall. Nearby, a steady stream of rusty water dripped from a small refrigerator. On its top the remains of a pot of beans still sat on a blackened hot plate. Several roaches were crawling up the wall. Behind the half-open door to the last room, a few gaudy dresses hung on nails, and a long blond wig had been thrown on top of a pile of old movie magazines.

During the search all three girls, dressed only in torn and stained underpants, wandered aimlessly around the room, muttering threats and curses. Just skin and bone, they looked more like leprous zombies than anything human. Their flanks were stringy and shriveled; their pathetic breasts, flat and pendulous. The backs of their arms, hips, and legs were covered with "track marks" (needle punctures), some were reddened, swelling, and ulcerated from using tincture of opium (when heroin was not available). Their hair was matted like old birds' nests and they stank. The third room held the only bed, its sagging mattress covered with grimy, cigarette-burned sheets, the pillow smeared with dark-red lipstick.

After their search, which netted several bags of heroin, a small amount of cocaine, and a couple of "joints" (marijuana cigarettes), the detectives told the girls to get dressed and began questioning each separately in the first bedroom. They hoped one of the girls would "cop a plea" (give incriminating information on the other suspects in order to get a recommendation of leniency from the arresting officer in court).

I first started traveling with the Narcotics Squad in 1962, and only on rare occasions did the addicts ever know I was a priest. My intention was not to rehabilitate, counsel, or work with the addicts directly. I was there to learn by observation—to collect first-hand data for my lectures and counseling of parents and children. Tonight for the first time we were trying out the procedure set up at the Bureau to give me maximum exposure to addicts and addiction without disclosing my identity. My cover name was "the lieutenant." When the detectives were finished questioning the addicts, they would say, "Now the lieutenant wants to ask you some questions." Then I would step in and quiz each one along these lines:

"How long have you been 'strung-out'?" (Length of time on drugs.)

"Are you 'joy-popping'?" (Injecting heroin or cocaine under the skin or in an abscess, also called "skin-popping.")

"Mainlining?" (Injecting heroin in a vein.)

"Snorting?" (Sniffing or inhaling heroin or cocaine.)

"What first turned you on to drugs?" (How did you begin to take drugs?)

"Blowing weed?" (Smoking pot.)

"Popping pills?" (Taking amphetamines and barbiturates.)

"Dropping acid?" (Taking LSD.)

"Why did you start?"

The first girl I questioned was Josie herself. She was twenty-eight and looked fifty. Somewhere in the past few years the warmth of her eyes had chilled. Now they were cold and tearless. Since there was no other place to sit in privacy, she led me back to the rear bedroom. Chain-smoking she told me to sit on the bed. Meanwhile, she strutted about the bare room in her blond wig, flicking ashes on the floor at random.

Just as I was about to ask her the first question, I heard a baby crying feebly. The cries seemed to be coming from under the bed. I bent down and pulled out a wet, stained corrugated carton. A tiny shriveled baby lay moaning on a few stinking rags. Closer examination revealed a twisted broken little arm. He was also raw and red from hardened excrement. The compulsive nature of addiction was getting through to me more and more. Nothing, absolutely nothing, matters when it conflicts with an addict's craving for drugs. The most basic ties of blood, love, responsibility, duty, pride are all luxuries of another life, of another world. All human considerations and niceties necessarily disappear. The being God created to be master of the universe with a glorious spiritual destiny becomes a voracious animal shackled to a destiny of satisfying the primitive needs of a steadily deteriorating body. This can be a very real and dismal legacy awaiting anyone who is willing to dabble irresponsibly in drugs.

When I asked Josie if she knew the baby's arm was broken, she flew into a shrill tirade. Gesturing wildly, she flung out strings of unintelligible phrases punctuated with four-letter words. Then she ran out of steam and began to cry. Between hoarse sobs Josie told me the baby was hers. She had dropped him yesterday afternoon after taking a fix.

"I picked him up off the bed to feed him just after I shot up. It must have been real good stuff, because all I wanted to do was fly around the room when the high hit me. I just forgot I was holding him. He fell, but I didn't even hear him crying. I just pulled on my new wig and that green dress and took off. When I came back today, I was so tired and hot, I just shoved him in the box and sacked-out. I didn't do it on purpose. I'm not that kind."

She stopped abruptly and looked toward the doorway. The sergeant had overheard Josie's noisy outburst. Fearing an attack on me or a suicide attempt, he had rushed to the back bedroom, interrupting his interrogation of the other two girls.

We wrapped the baby in some old T-shirts we found lying around and called for a patrol car to rush it to the hospital.

The next girl I talked to, Mollie, was far less coarse and arrogant than the other prostitutes. In a soft, almost shy brogue peculiarly laced with junkie slang she told me her story. She was the eldest of thirteen children born to a poor Catholic family in Londonderry, Ireland. It was a suffocating, strict, and joyless home—too little money, too many children.

"I was their servant, not their daughter. I wasn't allowed to bring home friends from school. I was never allowed to go out with boys. An ad in the Dublin paper advertised that a Catholic family in New York City would pay my fare to America and a monthly wage if I would sign a contract for two years as a mother's helper.

"The family I lived with were very good to me. They gave me two nights out a week. The freedom was so grand. Nothing to do but please myself. But then it all began to seem like the same old drudgery I ran away from. A month later in Central Park I met Greta, another mother's helper. Greta told me what a 'groove' the singles scene could be. I didn't even know the meaning of the words. She laughed and asked me to join her and her boyfriend at a pub on Second Avenue on my Thursday night out. For the first time in my life there was no one to tell me 'No.'

"I found the men in Greta's crowd liked me. Greta thought it was amusing to have a virgin in the crowd. One day in the park while we were watching the children, Greta gave me a few puffs of a special cigarette. It made me giggle and feel so strange. I even had a funny feeling when I looked at the men walking through the park. Greta said it was time I really learned about the sweet life, 'Time to torch up and turn on.'

"That night Greta's crowd had a 'blasting party' (pot party). . . . I 'blew' (smoked) four 'sticks' (marijuana cigarettes), and Greta's boyfriend taught me how to make love. At first I couldn't get enough 'pot' (marijuana) or sex. I never had one without the other. But then one of Greta's chums got pregnant and with my sex drive I got scared I might be the next. It's against my religious training to use birth control and besides I was getting very depressed. Such an empty life. All that messy business.

"Greta said the magic word was cocaine! She taught me to snort and later to joy-pop for a quicker high. We used to meet on our days off and sniff cocaine all afternoon. When it was over, I felt as if someone had washed my mind out and hung it out to dry in the sun! It was almost a religious experience. This complete release was like . . . like receiving absolution in confession!

"By this time I was starting to have problems with my employers because I stayed out all night on my days off. I was extremely nervous and began to have trouble controlling the children. Greta and I even used to skin-pop in Central Park while the kids played.

One day she told me she had a new 'connection' who wanted her to let him give a works party at her apartment. That's where I learned to mainline heroin. At first I didn't need much, but within two weeks my monthly salary was barely enough to buy one week's 'fixes.' I had been buying all my heroin through Greta, and thought she just bought enough 'junk' for the two of us. But it turned out Greta was a 'dealer' and when I ran out of money I found my credit was no good with her.

"Greta wasn't laughing when she said: 'You always told

me that you'd love to make the bastards pay!' I quit my job on three days' notice and moved in with Greta. Look at me. I'm eighteen years old. In the past six months I've lived in a worse hell than anything I heard from the nuns in parochial school. I'm glad it's all over. I'm glad I've been caught."

This was my first meeting with addict-prostitutes. It would not be my last. I was to see many heartbreaking things in the days to come as I traveled with the squad. The ravages worked on the addicts' wasted bodies were devestatingly thorough.

I thought of the movies I had seen on drugs, of the TV shows—each one of them trying to be realistic. But how easy it is to miss the point when they usually have a "Raquel Welch" playing a junkie-prostitute and a "Steve McQueen" portraying an addict. Young people seeing such a show are almost necessarily apt to remark, "Well, now, the drug habit can't be all that bad!" If they could only see the genuine article, the broken creature who soaks up drugs like a sponge. The visual shock and aroma might have a more sobering impact.

I couldn't understand how these girls, looking as they did, could possibly make any money as prostitutes. It seemed that only the most unbelievably frustrated could even consider them sexually, and pay them money in the bargain. The detectives explained that they usually did their hustling around bars at about two or three in the morning when all the customers were just about blind drunk. Wearing a wig, perfume, and enough clothes, powder, and makeup in the right places to cover a multitude of sins, they could do very well.

Before I could talk with Greta, the detectives asked the girls to get ready to go to the police station. As I looked at these three withered figures, I thought how adept man is in destroying the works of God. It is sad to see polluted streams; tons of cement where grass, trees, and flowers used to be; smokestacks fouling the pure air. But there is nothing more depressing and tragic than to witness the human body, one of His greatest creations, so desecrated.

Sullen and hostile, the women got into the police car. And I wondered who or what in this world was the most accountable for the tragic foul-up of these three lives.

2
History

During the nineteenth century a salty character drove his horse and wagon over the bumpy trails on the western frontier. His arrival in any town was always a big event. While peddling chewing tobacco, saddlesoap, belts, pins, and bright, printed cloth, he regaled his audience with spellbinding tales of his magic elixir—"snake oil"!

But to some he was more than idle entertainment. He was a necessity, and the time between visits was long and painful. When he left town, their dyspepsia and rheumatism became unbearable. For they were the hopeless junkies of yesterday, and he was the pioneer pusher, whose magic elixir was basically opium. Ironically, he was often an innocent victim of his own snake oil. He didn't intend to encourage drug addiction any more than the corner apothecary in the big cities. Yet they both supplied the means to this end with their potent, patent painkillers and their "youth" tonics.

It was not unusual during the Victorian era to see a prim and proper lady mince into an apothecary shop in her neighborhood to buy a patent nerve tonic and then go home and get "stoned." And who can forget Mark Twain's vivid and hilarious description of Aunt Polly's cat after Tom Sawyer fed him a whole bottle of "painkiller"?

How long has marijuana been on the scene? A certain insidious plant grew in wild clumps on the plains of the southwestern United States and Mexico. Mexican ranch hands of the 1860s and '70s called it locoweed because of the maddening effect it had on horses and cattle who ate it while grazing. Ranchers gave strict orders to shoot all such unfortunate animals before they hurt themselves or ran amuck in the herd.

Peyote and mescaline, now part of the equipment of the weekend "tripper," were, for the previous 400 years, sacred ceremonial hallucinogens used by the Plains Indians of North America. Indian priests and seers used the highly intoxicating distillate of the mescal cactus to induce visions of the future and to talk with distant gods.

There were no laws governing the sale of narcotics before the Pure Food and Drug Act of 1909. Indeed, the home medical books of the eighteenth and nineteenth centuries advised the unsuspecting rheumatic and arthritic to rub laudanum (tincture of opium) liberally into the painful, swelling joints for quick relief from pain. In addition, the sufferer was to take several large spoonfuls daily by mouth. And, lazy nursemaids were often guilty of addicting innocent babies under six months of age to opium. It was so easy to slip a little laudanum into baby's milk and so nice not to hear him cry all night. Or day.

By the late 1800s there were over 300,000 known addicts in the United States. When the hypodermic needle was introduced, doctors gave injections of a new opium derivative—morphine—for almost any disorder. Because of the lack of proper anesthetics during the Civil War, many veterans returned to civilian life addicted to morphine. This problem of addiction was believed to be solved forever when a doctor in Germany developed another opium derivative—heroin. This drug, heralded in the early medical journals as being nonaddictive and safe, tragically proved to be about five times more addictive than morphine.

In Austria during the 1880s young Dr. Sigmund Freud was one of the first physicians to recognize the local anesthetic properties of a new drug from South America and the West Indies—cocaine, a derivative of the leaves of the shrub coca. Freud used it daily for his chronic indigestion, even mailing some of the powder to his fiancée and his family for use as a general tonic.

South American Indians for centuries had chewed these leaves to deaden feelings of hunger and cold. Soon Swiss and English doctors were widely touting cocaine's local-anesthetic properties for delicate operations on the eyes, abdominal hernias, and clubfeet. Although less addictive than morphine and heroin, within a few years cocaine also proved a mixed blessing. Better than half of the post-operative cases became seriously addicted, some even progressing to the harder drugs, morphine and heroin.

During this same era, reports from the great social centers in London and Paris claimed that sniffing cocaine at the theater increased one's enjoyment of the play.

Throughout history the drug problem has been excused, disguised, and hidden. Today, society is at last beginning to accept the painful responsibility of dealing with the addict and his problem.

Today's addict is not a total loss. He does serve someone—he's the one who keeps the drinks coming around the pools in expensive hotels, provides big houses, chauffeur-driven cars, fast women, and sweet-smoking cigars for the fat cats of international organized crime. These big smugglers and wholesalers who keep the narcotics trade brisk are almost impossible to touch: Teams of expensive lawyers provide them with the mobility of legitimate business. Driven to support their habit, addicts steal from $10,000,000 to $15,000,000 each day in the United States alone, turning over the cash they get from "fences" to organized crime for narcotics. Unfortunately, the narcotics operations of most police departments have dealt only with the least important and the most visible elements of the world-wide narcotics syndicate—the local dealer and the street "pusher."

A dealer might sell between 50 and 100 bags of heroin a day. If the street price to the pusher for a "nickel bag" is $5.00, then this dealer is taking in between $250 and $500 daily. "Busting" a dealer only temporarily dries up a neighborhood. In a few days another dealer will take up where the busted one left off. This knowledge is frustrating and difficult to accept, but the police continue to make every possible effort to stem the flow of heroin and other drugs from foreign countries, primarily France and Turkey.

Under the anti-drug laws of the recent past the emphasis has always been placed upon removal of the addict from society as if he were a criminal. Today the drug problem is so widespread that the emphasis is shifting from indiscriminate imprisonment to individual rehabilitation. The combined forces of the professions of medicine, psychology, and sociology are at last focusing on the work of prevention through mass education and upon rehabilitation programs. Parents must avidly support these educational narcotics programs in the schools their children attend. Civic-minded citizens everywhere must insist that properly supervised rehabilitation centers—sponsored by local and federal government agencies as well as private foundations and reinforced by continued and intensified research by qualified personnel—are set up as soon as possible in every city.

I firmly believe that legalization of marijuana would be

a naïve and dangerous action. However, the nonpenal approach for teen-agers caught for the first time smoking or possessing marijuana is a more realistic approach to the problem. We must face the fact that there are a lot of teen-agers who will experiment with marijuana at least once. They are not criminals, but if we treat them as such, we may drive them into a criminal pattern. When I say treat them as criminals, I mean charging them with a felony which, if conviction follows, excludes them from the possibility of becoming a doctor, lawyer, or legislator; it even excludes them from the privilege of voting. In my mind, here is a case where the punishment does not fit the crime.

Furthermore, while strong consideration should be given toward lessening the penalty for possession and use of marijuana, the penalty for those who deal and push should be tremendously stiffened. There is no law against *being* an addict; there is only a law against *possessing* narcotics illegally. The Federal Food, Drug & Cosmetic Act passed in 1965 and amended in 1968 states:

> Anyone who possesses dangerous drugs illegally is subject to a penalty of not more than one year imprisonment and/or a $1,000 fine for a first or second offense, and not more than three years imprisonment and/or a $10,000 fine for a third offense. However, the offender may be placed on probation for the first offense. If he meets the condition of his probation the court may set aside his conviction. A second offense allows for probation, but the conviction may not be set aside. An offense of possession with intent to sell, manufacture, or sale of dangerous drugs is subject to a penalty of not more than five years imprisonment and/or a $10,000 fine. There are special penalties for violators over eighteen years of age who sell or give drugs to anyone under twenty-one years old. For a

first offense the punishment may be imprisonment for not more than ten years and/or a fine of $15,000. A second offense carries a penalty of not more than fifteen years imprisonment and/or a fine of $20,000.

Only a few states have what they call "Internal Possession Law," which means: If an addict has just had a fix, he is considered to be illegally possessing narcotics internally and is subject to arrest. Contrary to what you may have heard, in my experience with the New York Narcotics Squad I felt it was not the objective of the police to arrest or harass every poor junkie that came across their path. Their primary concern is focused on ways and means of entrapping the big wholesaler and dealer.

Under present federal and state laws, those convicted of narcotics felonies stand to lose the following rights and privileges:

1. The right to vote.
2. The right to run for public office.
3. The right to become a licensed:
   doctor, dentist, CPA, attorney, architect, realtor, pharmacist, school teacher, private detective, barber . . . and many other career opportunities.
4. The right to own firearms—pistols, rifles, or shotguns.
5. The right to work for the city, state, or federal government.
6. The right to be admitted to West Point, Annapolis, the Air Force Academy, or the Merchant Marine Academy. If you enlist in the service, you do not have a choice of which branch you are placed in. You may not hold commissioned rank.

In addition to the loss of these rights and privileges is the ostracism of family, friends, and society. Considering these irreversible consequences as well as the permanent mental and physical damage drugs can cause, it is extraordinary that anyone considers drugs as "just experimenting" or has any hesitation in answering the question, "Is it worth it?" Only gross irresponsibility would allow God-given life to be treated in such cavalier fashion.

3

Symptoms

Your son may be doing a very creditable job in school. Besides studies, he is involved in sports, clubs, and the usual round of activities that keep high schoolers busy and out of trouble. Then you begin to notice, in small ways at first, that he is becoming lazy. When you mention this to him, his attitude is one of indifference rather than defiance. The activities and hobbies that previously absorbed all his waking moments are now ignored. He just isn't interested. Do his eyes look a little glazed now and then? Have his study sessions at home become a rarity and has his school work taken a nosedive? Marijuana can become such an all-engrossing habit that interest in other things dwindles or only receives mediocre attention.

Has his vocabulary suddenly become very hip? Whereas before, he may have used the usual glib slang of the day, are his conversations now laced with the jargon of the pot scene? Words like "stick," or "joint," "torch up" (light a marijuana cigarette), "blow grass," "blasting party," "tea head" or "pot head" (regular pot smoker), "roach" or "jefferson airplane" (butt end of a marijuana cigarette held by a pin or paper clip) might betray a more than casual acquaintance with marijuana.

Has his appetite increased greatly? Does he, like a pregnant woman, have sudden cravings for exotic snacks at odd hours? Have his compliments on your cooking become unusually flowery? Marijuana alone in the drug scene sharply increases the desire for food and makes the sense of taste extremely keen.

The home-rolled marijuana cigarette or the aluminum-foil–lined pipe are obvious and incriminatory—you are not likely to find these lying around his room. But have you noticed an unusually pungent, incense-like odor of smoke in his clothes? When you vacuumed his rug yesterday, did you overlook some tiny seeds caught in the tangled fringes? Did you brush some dried leaf particles off his dresser top with your dustcloth? When you sent his sports jacket to the cleaners this morning, did you find some fine gray-green crumbs in the pocket that looked like catnip or oregano? Did you detect the unmistakeable signs of a "hang-over" depression when he left for school this morning—but he went to bed early last night and there's no beer or liquor missing from your supply and no empties in his room? Many adults, especially high-strung, creative types, experience a definite low the day after a night of high-flying on pot. Think about the effect of such depressions on the immature teen-ager, whose moods are mercurial under the most ideal circumstances.

Most teenagers exposed to marijuana don't know what to believe about the drug. They rarely know the origin or potency of what they're smoking: catnip; oregano; Vietnamese, Mexican, or California marijuana—or a hashish-opium mix from Turkey. It all goes under the loose heading of pot. The dealer and the pusher are not concerned with the user's welfare.

Think about the groovy kid down the block who "totaled" his new GTO convertible last Saturday night on the concrete bridge abutment—six teen-agers were riding with him—four are dead, one is blind, and one will never walk without crutches. The groovy kid was lucky—he only lost one arm. He thought the car was a jet plane, and they were all singing as he took off over the river. Would you like to face him on the highway late at night as he's coming home from a blasting party? Or at noon as you are carrying your groceries across an intersection in Anytown, USA? Teen-age highway fatalities resulting from abuse of pot, hashish, or pills are a new addition to our "cool" national pastime called statistics.

Leaving the realm of marijuana and stepping into the "spaced-out" (vague and incoherent) world of the hallucinogens—LSD, mescaline, and peyote—took us to Washington Square Park. The detectives were looking for an informer, well-known to the Narcotics Squad, who had agreed to help them close down a Village bar trafficking in junk. As it happened, we came across a small band of hippies kneeling in a circle on the grass chanting the ancient Hindu ritual "Oome Padme Hum." In the center of the circle a slender, long-haired brunette of about seventeen sat in the lotus position rocking back and forth to their rhythmic chant. Though it was a cool evening—about sixty degrees—she was naked except for a beaded loincloth and an Indian headband covered with little silver bells. From time to time she burst into rhapsodic descriptions of God.

> "Oh see! My blood is green fire! Touch me, God! Touch me! He walks with stars shoes through my eyes!
> Listen! He sings to me in my crystal bones. . . . Oome padme hummmm——"

Holding the note, letting the vibrations fill her head and body with orgasmic sensations, she lapsed into silence and assumed a trancelike state.

The detectives broke up the group of hippies, who sauntered off on various paths, still chanting. Then they helped the girl to her feet. Her pupils appeared to be extremely dilated and her body was covered with gooseflesh from the cold. She didn't resist when they helped her put on a long white Indian *kurta,* which had been lying on the grass beside her. No matter what the detectives asked her she whispered disjointed phrases and made odd clucking noises with her tongue. Frustrated in our efforts to establish her identity and address, we looked in her leather shoulder pouch, which was lying on a nearby park bench. There was a letter addressed to "Valerie" on Park Avenue in the Seventies. We drove uptown and parked in front of a luxury apartment house. When the doorman came to the car, he spoke to Valerie by name and directed us to 19-B.

We rang the bell for a long time. The door was finally opened by a disheveled, sleepy-eyed woman in a lace negligee. The minute she saw Valerie she launched into a tirade and demanded to know if we were taking her daughter to jail. The detectives patiently explained that we had picked Valerie up for indecent exposure and suspicion of possession of drugs in Washington Square Park. They made it clear that next time they or other Narcotics Squad detectives would have to take more drastic action. Totally oblivious to her mother's ranting, Valerie shuffled into the living room and flopped on the sofa. Her mother told us she would call Valerie's father—her ex-husband—immediately. We left the mother shouting and threatening her daughter, who sat smiling and clucking to herself. We had given Valerie's mother the names of several public and private agencies where counsel and treatment were available in Manhattan. On the way down in the elevator I wondered if she would contact any of them.

Suppose Valerie was your daughter. How would you know she was using a hallucinogenic drug and was not just drunk? The signs of LSD use, like those of marijuana, are difficult to spot. LSD ("acid") is colorless, odorless, and tasteless—but so are grain alcohol and vodka. Valerie was heavily drugged and demonstrated the effects more noticeably. Impressionable teen-agers like her have been told by some hip-sounding "acid-head" that LSD frees the mind and gives you deep, so-called personal insights. . . . You may even, like Valerie, believe you are talking directly with God. Some acid-heads like to make the ritual of "dropping acid" even more meaningful—by liquifying it and pouring it into their eye sockets.

Scrambled sensory impressions and wild converging colors can flood the mind of a person tripping with LSD, DMT, STP, mescaline, or peyote. Reactions are extremely unpredictable—sound becomes color, cold becomes hot, liquid becomes solid. Limitations and boundaries disappear. I saw the waterlogged body of a teen-age girl that police fished out of a swimming pool during a graduation party—her classmates told me she was convinced she was a fish and could breathe under water. I saw another teenager on a stretcher in Bellevue Hospital screaming incoherently and hemorrhaging—he had driven steel needles into the pupils of his eyes so the beauties of his soul could shine through.

Both during and after a trip your son or daughter will lose his appetite completely. In addition, even if he has had a good trip and has not "wigged-out" or "freaked-out" (had a bad trip—and retired from the scene with a shattered nervous system) the aftermath of anxiety and depression can radically disturb his metabolism, causing it to burn up energy (glycogen—sugar stored in the liver) at an abnormally rapid rate. The result in most cases will be a dramatic weight loss.

Has your son's or daughter's usually happy and even disposition undergone any changes lately? Is he or she acting high-strung, edgy, and argumentative for no apparent reason? Do you lie in bed some nights and hear your son or daughter tossing and turning or sleeplessly prowling his room? Repeated use of hallucinogens—and this includes amphetamines as well as LSD, peyote, mescaline, and the synthetics DMT and STP—often leaves a teenager panic-stricken, filled with abnormal guilts and fears that prevent him from sleeping. He becomes spaced-out. Without help, the mounting pressures from these anxieties and the external pressures of daily life may force him into a radical personality change. He may try snorting cocaine or mainlining heroin in an effort to escape his unbearable tensions—just to get by from day to day. Antisocial and even criminal behavior may result.

Prolonged and serious psychotic states such as acute schizophrenia are often the gruesome legacy of a bad trip. The fragile equilibrium of our sanity hangs from such a delicate thread that freaking-out can snap the slender twist of filaments into a thousand frayed ends. There are no known miracle drugs which can instantly splice them together. Again and again, users have reported the frightening phenomenon of suddenly "tripping-out" (hallucinating) weeks or even months after they had last taken LSD. It can happen anywhere and any time—while driving the car, while swimming in the ocean, while having an interview for your first job.

The dangers of experimenting with the hallucinogens cannot be overstressed. One single ounce has sufficient potency to send thousands of users on a trip for several hours. One tiny speck of LSD disolved in any food or drink serves the purpose. Indeed students sometimes mail LSD to each other under the postage stamp on the envelope. Because of its undetectability I always caution teen-agers, especially girls, never to accept *any* soft drink in a public place unless they see the bottle being opened and watch it being poured. Even then you have no guarantees that the drink hasn't been doctored. This precaution is especially necessary at large public dances, rock festivals, at the beach, and anywhere large groups of teen-agers congregate. Indeed, college students at some of the major New York colleges and universities have been turned on to acid by some of their teachers and professors.

You as a parent may know all the symptoms, dangers, and effects of LSD abuse—in the abstract—but unless you know your son or daughter very well, his or her addiction may escape your notice. Your best safeguards against the nightmare of addiction are frank and open communication between you and your child and careful, long-term observation of his behavior pattern. Any sudden and repeated deviations from his norm may be the danger signals of LSD abuse.

One night in the wake of two narcotics detectives I jostled my way through a crowd of gawking pedestrians and walked through the door of a poolroom. A huge mountain of a man lay face up and spread-eagled in the middle of the floor—350 pounds of flaccid, greasy flesh squashed against the floor like a beached whale. A few poolsharks stood near a wall, trying to look cool and inconspicuous. No one would admit knowing him—who he was or where he lived. No one wanted to risk being busted. The ambulance attendant thought the man had probably died of an "O.D." (overdose) of pills or heroin. . . . The track marks on his arms indicated that he was a long-term user of heroin. One of the detectives walked to the rear of the poolroom to check a back door. And in a few seconds he returned herding a boy of about fifteen in faded Levi's and a filthy T-shirt, which hung stiffly over his boney shoulders like a shroud. He exhibited all the classic symptoms of long-time heroin addiction—red-rimmed, light-sensitive eyes, runny nose, emaciated body, and nervous behavior. The three plastic bags of uncut heroin found in his pants pocket confirmed that he was a junkie. During interrogation, Tony admitted riffling the pockets of the fat man—a small-scale dealer—as he lay dying.

Now, suppose this young mainliner was your son (or daughter)? Would you have known he was shooting heroin? Could you have second-guessed him soon enough? Could you have prevented him from getting so strung-out that he started rolling addicts and corpses to get a fix?

The indications of drug abuse can be very subtle in the apprentice junkie. Because the first stages of drug abuse often dovetail with the frenetic pace of everyday living, they can go undetected for a long time. At the time, the unsuspecting parents tolerate and absorb all the aggravation, the disruption of household schedules, the irrational behavior, strange dress, and slovenly habits as part of the hectic, whirlwind life of the teen-ager. In retrospect, any parent of an addict can tell you that when you add up all the seemingly innocent aggravations and episodes, the total often equals addiction.

Once the stark reality of drug abuse is present, a parent discovers ruefully that his child's innocence is only one more stratagem to cover his addiction, to play for time, for money. Addicts brag that they are the best actors and liars in the world. One young addict told me whenever her parents accused her of using drugs, she would cry with deep heaving sobs and watch her parents melt—they always reproached themselves bitterly for doubting her. She had also convinced her mother that the track marks on her arms were spider bites. These stratagems always seemed to work until the day her mother was sorting the soiled laundry and found a disposable plastic hypo tucked under the foam-rubber pad in a strapless bra.

Maybe your son has always been solidly built, and, like most teen-agers, extremely body-conscious—preferring his T-shirts to be tight to accentuate his well-defined muscles. Then, for some curious reason, he becomes extremely modest in his dress. You notice, but chalk it up to another fad. Long-sleeved shirts are now his favorite. He gets unduly annoyed if someone walks in on him in the bathroom while he's shaving in T-shirt and shorts. His bathing suit has been hanging in the laundry room unused for weeks. People who are mainlining heroin are always very self-conscious about the visible track marks left by the needle and the abscesses and scabs from skin-popping with an old safety pin.

As in the case of other types of drug abuse, your child's studies are immediately affected. He can't concentrate on homework, won't answer in class, begins to fail tests. He no longer takes any interest in sports competition. He comes home with the prefabricated story that someone stole his new transistor out of his locker. Translation: He sold it to a fence near school for fix money. In fact, he may suddenly become tremendously careless about leaving things around to be stolen.

Has it been a long time since you heard him joke or kid about his girlfriends? Heroin diminishes sexual drive. Consequently, the physical or sexual attraction that motivates the start of a wholesome male-female relationship is absent.

Does your teen-ager seem to be walking around in his sleep, with a slack jaw and eyelids so heavy he can't seem to keep them open? When questioned, is he evasive and uncommunicative? Does he try to gloss over any situation in which he might have to exert himself with: "Just can't hack it, Dad. I'm too beat from the grind at school." Is he just "too beat" to enjoy that neighborhood game of touch football? Does he call it a stupid kid's game and say it's no groove?

Has he stopped appearing regularly for meals, claiming he's lost his appetite? Complete obsession and preoccupation with drugs, especially heroin, excludes any type of normal eating or sleeping. The natural result of this is severe malnutrition and physical weakness. The user's body eventually becomes extremely vulnerable to diseases such as mononucleosis, pneumonia, T.B., syphilis, and severe kidney malfunction—such diseases, serious in a healthy person, often mean death to the addict, whose resistance is low or nonexistent.

Suppose one day you walk into your son's or daughter's room and find a minor miracle—his bed is made. The squalid "pad" is clean and orderly. Would you suspect him or trust him? An addict once told me that he used to hide his set of works in the springs of his bed. He didn't want his mother to accidentally find his cache as she tucked in the sheets and blankets, so he started making his own bed. If you then accidentally discovered your child's set of works, would you realize what you were looking at? [A set of works includes a hollow hypodermic needle, a syringe of some type (usually an eyedropper), a spoon or bottle cap in which to cook (disolve) the heroin, and possibly a rubber tourniquet (to tie off the circulation and force a vein to the surface)—though his belt or her nylon stocking would do. Warning! This kit does not include a disinfectant such as rubbing alcohol. If your teen-ager should spread the word that he's having a works party that weekend you planned to be away overnight, don't be surprised at the unwelcome guests who may linger—virulent bacterial infections such as hepatitis, staph, and strep. For the host supplies his works in return for a taste of each guest's heroin supply. And ten or fifteen kids, some clean, some seriously diseased, may shoot it up with the same filthy needle.]

A teen-ager is playing double Russian roulette every time he takes a fix. There is no way he can gauge the percentage content of heroin in each fix, nor can he ever be sure what type of bulk powder the dealer has used to "cut" his supply. Each addict's system tolerates a different percentage of heroin. Mainlining a stronger mixture is courting death from an overdose. When police seizure of large quantities of heroin in a given district causes a panic in the streets, the dealer will use any powder that comes readily to hand to stretch his dwindling supplies—fatally toxic substances such as Ajax and Bonami cleansers and borated baby powder, or harmless sugar and cornstarch.

Junkies, fearing a bust, will not call a doctor or the police when a fellow addict shoots up an overdose. Instead, they may try several useless and/or fatal home remedies:

1. They will inject milk in his veins. (Doctors claim this is useless.)
2. They will force milk down his throat. (Useless and sometimes fatal; if the addict is lucky, he will only have a painful session of vomiting; if he is unlucky, he may drown when the milk floods his lungs.)
3. They will inject a salt solution in his vein. (The resulting jolt may cause a heart attack.)

In case of extreme toxicity (as in any case of poisoning) or possible overdose of narcotics the best plan is to call the police department and your family physician immediately.

Caution! All of these external indications of addiction only make sense and warrant consideration when they are kept within the context of an existing problem situation.

4

Keep Off the Grass

You can almost smell the dope in Harlem. A detective who had been there posing as a junkie invited two "narcs" and me to a pot party.

No stage could have been more perfectly set, no scene more vividly designed to depict the gruesome drama of drug abuse. As we drove through Harlem, every corner was bustling with activity: ramshackle houses spitting kids into the street, winos stuffed into doorways, steamed-up windows on greasy-spoon diners, storefront churches three to a block.

Within a few minutes we left the main drag and were slowly moving down a dark, deserted side street. One of the detectives turned to me saying, "Don't get shook, Father, we should be picking up our contact any second now." No sooner were the words out of his mouth, than a shadowy figure darted from between two old buildings, jerked open the back door of the car, and slipped in beside me.

"Whew! I thought you guys would never come. I just left a knife scene, man. A couple of junkies were going to do a little cutting on a pusher who sold them some 'dummies.' I split fast."

Our contact, Mark, was a young Negro detective. And because in Harlem a black man in a car with three white men is immediately suspect, he kept down and well out of sight. His assignment was very risky, and detection by addicts could bring him serious physical harm, even death, especially if they thought he was consorting with the police, or "gray cats" as white policemen are sometimes known in Harlem.

Mark and I talked about a lot of things, although, strangely enough, not about drugs. I almost fell out of the car when he told me he was reading the life of Pope Pius X. But as we continued talking about his wife and children it became obvious he was a devout Catholic.

As we approached the neighborhood where the pot party was being held, Mark slipped out of the car. He had given us the address, and we would join him there later—after the guests were all high and our presence would not be noticed in the mixed gathering.

It was ten-thirty P.M. The party was supposed to have started at eight o'clock. This was a so-called classy affair—no strung-out junkies were invited.

We parked the car in a nearby alley, and one detective and I hurried toward the house. The other detective and some other police would come in later when the bust was in full swing. He was going to give us five minutes inside, unless we blew the whistle sooner. Two squad cars were lying in wait just a couple of blocks away.

As we approached the tenement, we saw some people going in a side entrance. That saved us from making the mistake of heading straight for the front door, although there was no doubt we were at the right address: In front of the doorway a girl was standing barefooted atop a fire hydrant doing gymnastic exercises—stoned out of her mind. We opened the door and found ourselves in a long dimly lit hallway. The stink of urine and other human waste hit us full force. Later on I found out there was only one working toilet in the hall for the entire house. Gracious ghetto living.

The party had overflowed into the hallway, where a guy was scrawling obscene graffiti on the wall. My initial curiosity started to wane, and I began wishing it was all over. "Just look cool, Father." At this point, that was like trying to tell an elephant to hide in a breadbox.

When we reached the door the detective opened it and we stepped inside. I felt a hand reach up and grab my arm. It scared the hell out of me. What a relief when I looked down and saw it was my "Pius X" friend! The detective and I slumped down against the wall, and I watched in amazement. The room was lit with candles, and it gave the appearance of being crowded with featureless silhouettes, a shadowy specter of souls rather than bodies. The smoke was so thick you could get high without burning a joint.

Some people had clothes on, some people didn't. Others looked like they couldn't make up their minds. The guests were black and white, with a few visitors from Chinatown. Some of the pot smokers were getting to know themselves and each other through "group grope." One guy was strumming his guitar while singing and emoting. Others were undulating to their own rhythm and beat. Everyone was immersed in his own thing. (No one seemed really interested in anybody else.) It must have been yoga night judging from the girl outside and the flaked-out guy I was now watching over in a corner wearing only long strands of silver beads, he sat straight-backed and sat motionless with his legs wrapped around his neck.

I noticed a black man with one of those classic faces—a strong, yet soft, expression. All the features were transmitting in one look the entire idea of "Black Pride." He reached under a heavy sweater and took out a piece of cigarette and a small glassine envelope. Once or twice he met my stare, and I looked away as nonchalantly as I could. I watched as he carefully shook out a small amount of what I guessed was marijuana and then spread it evenly with his finger. He rolled it tight and squashed in the ends, so as not to lose any, and leaned over and got a light from a candle burning on a small table. He took two quick, long drags, sucking the smoke deep into his lungs. He held his breath for a few seconds before passing the joint to the girl next to him. Then leaning back, he closed his eyes and waited for the high.

Suddenly the lights came on and made me squint. I knew it was time to move, but I didn't know where. People were tripping over my feet trying to get out of the apartment. The raid was in full swing, and I dashed to what I figured a neutral corner. Some of the people jumped out the windows and I wondered if they wouldn't have done the same thing if we were on the third floor. They ran right into the arms of waiting policemen stationed outside. Sprained ankles and whoozy equilibrium stopped any getaway attempts. I counted about eighteen people.

A pup tent was pitched in the corner of the room. We never did know why, but later we finally came up with an explanation that seemed to satisfy everyone—most likely it was the host's private boudoir for entertaining the ladies. A few ratty mattresses on top of ripped-up cardboard boxes were scattered around, and a peace sign was on the wall. Evidence of marijuana was everywhere. I saw at least four or five "roaches" (the butt ends of marijuana cigarettes) on the floor. Users hold roaches with toothpicks, pins, and paper clips to smoke the butts down as far as possible. Marijuana becomes stronger the closer you get to the butt. A search turned up two full bags of marijuana, one stuffed down into a shoe and the other in the empty tank above the smelly toilet in the hallway.

We headed for the police station. At the station quarrelsome and obscene comments greeted the detectives as everyone lined up against the wall. Of the crowd of eighteen, only seven were arrested. Two of them were the expected pushers—the real reason for the bust. In keeping with the usual Narcotics Squad tactics, Mark was one of those arrested. He played his part as a sullen, uncooperative junkie with great conviction. A good undercover agent with a well-developed network of underworld connections rarely makes the arrest himself. Being busted with the other potheads protects his cover and improves his usefulness for future operations.

A short while later at the police station I tried to talk with one of the eighteen year old boys, who had just been busted.

"How long have you been blowing pot?"

"About a year."

"What does it do for you?"

"Enough."

"What does that mean?"

"It's hard to explain, man."

"Do you know why you smoke pot?"

"Maybe I don't want to be a hung-up phony. I like it . . . who knows. . . .Why do you drink booze?"

"Do you think everybody is a phony?"

"Who knows . . . there's enough to go around."

"Are you going to continue to smoke pot?"

"Sure, why not?"

Before I could continue, a boy who was sitting on the floor a few feet away from us broke in, "Don't you want to know why I smoke pot, man? . . . I smoke pot because its the next best thing to getting screwed!"

With that he put his head back against the wall and

stared dreamily into space. His buddy next to him looked up at me saying, "Man, its beautiful. . . .When I turn on a record and listen to music and then light up a joint, I don't hear it. . . .I swallow it . . . I chew it . . . I mean, its all over me, man.

He smiled slightly, obviously relishing the sounds of each word. Propped against the bench nearby, a lanky girl with a matted brown hair continuously scrubbed her reddened eyes with dirty fingers as if to make the scene disappear. I asked her if pot had helped her to find herself. She interrupted my question angrily, exclaiming, "Who're you kidding! What d'ya mean, find yourself? All this business about grass helping you to know yourself is bull! How can you do that when all you do is talk to yourself, then giggle your ass off for a couple of hours!"

Admittedly, this pot party turned out to be raunchy. However, it doesn't make any difference if you tell me that the parties where you swing are innocent affairs with cool people. This may be true, but there is always someone around who wants to go a little further. You may not encounter this person during your first experience with marijuana. You might be lucky enough to avoid such an encounter over a long period of time. But eventually you will meet, and this certain someone could quite possibly be just the person you want to impress, and who impresses you. So, when he or she suggests something a little stronger than marijuana just for laughs, you don't want to be a drag, so you drop a little acid, shoot a little speed, pop a few pills, or snort a little heroin. I know—you would never go along with such a suggestion. Others have said that before you, with just as much determination, who will live to regret their foolhardiness the rest of their addict lives.

I looked at the four I had spoken to and then looked around at the rest of the kids busted in the raid. An all-pervading hopelessness was written on their faces. So many believe to keep up the struggle is useless. They see two worlds, one in the ghetto and one outside. Rising above the poverty and misery seems an impossible task. The resort to drugs to escape their bleak existence. I agonized with them, as in a few minutes I would agonize with some of their parents.

Being a parent today is the most difficult vocation in the world. *They* certainly aren't to blame for everything their children do. They are not always the bad guys. I have had the burden of telephoning parents the sad news that their son or daughter had been picked up on a marijuana charge. I have walked into my office and encountered that apprehensive look a parent has when they know exactly what you are going to say. And a question that always seems to come up is: "Why aren't they afraid of it, Father? After all they've been told about it, what it can possibly lead to—the dangers involved—why aren't they afraid of it?"

One reason is that youth has little or no fears about future possibilities; they are concerned for the most part with the present. Something drastic is always going to happen to the next guy, but never to them. To penetrate that barrier of youthful fearlessness is an uphill struggle, but parents must take the time and make the effort to listen and try to understand. So many people have something to sell today, so many are fanatically pushing a cause, so many are filled with a neurotic obsession to be heard. Gifted with a self-styled charisma, some people are always ready, able, and obliged to straighten you out. But nobody has time to listen. If we did, the generation gap would not be such a chasm. Even the young people, immersed as they are in the crusade for communication, have forgotten the art of listening. We are becoming a generation of finger-shakers shouting, "What you oughta do . . . !"

For this reason it is difficult to live in an age of reformers.

Important issues become buried under a mountain of blaring, insignificant ones. As a result, people stop listening, even to the important things. I prayed that night that young people, especially, will take time out to stop and listen. The entire story of marijuana has not yet been told. This should be enough to make us play it straight until science can tell us that it is harmful or harmless with true, reliable, and convincing evidence.

5

Broken Dreams

The day was a typical mid-July scorcher. A day that demanded long cool drinks, gushing fire hydrants, and the Good Humor man. The lucky ones were at the beach. I was cruising around Manhattan in a Narcotics Squad car with two detectives.

The steaming streets were bursting with young kids deaf to the groans of heat-sick adults. Shopkeepers stood in their doorways trying to find a little breeze while watching future Mickey Mantles play ball in garbage-strewn lots. Crudely drawn hopscotch squares lined the sidewalks, frisbees sailed aimlessly overhead, dogs and children darted in and out among the parked cars, and lines of gray laundry stretched between the dismal Lower Eastside tenements.

We stopped at a red light. Suddenly one of the detectives pointed to a boy crossing the street in front of us. "There goes junk."

The boy wore paint-spattered dungarees, high-top sneakers, and a white basketball jacket. He had a purposeful walk, but his scrawny hangdog appearance told us he was up to no good. We pulled over to the curb and let the motor idle as we watched him hurry down the block. "It's junk all right," the detective continued. "He's either a pusher making a 'drop' or an addict trying to 'score.' "

Halfway down the block the boy stopped, did a sort of shuffling step to avoid a little girl jumping rope, and took out a cigarette. He lit it and smoked it slowly, deliberately. He began moving nervously back and forth from foot to foot. Then, just as deliberately, he dropped the cigarette to the sidewalk and ground it out with his heel. He walked slowly past two more houses, turned, and disappeared into a hallway.

Tiny beads of sweat trickled down our faces, and my clothes stuck to the hot leather seat.

"There he is!" said one of the detectives suddenly as the boy reappeared. "We'll just let him walk a while," mused the detective who was driving. "If he's got junk, he hasn't stashed it yet. It's still in his hand. If we move in too fast, he might be able to get rid of it without us seeing it and he'll come up clean when we search him."

Again the boy stopped, lit a cigarette, shifted his weight briefly, and continued down the block. We gave him a couple of minutes and then tailed him for another block. Without warning the car accelerated, we pulled up alongside of him, and the two detectives jumped out as the car stopped short. The boy started to run, but he wasn't fast enough. After a brief scuffle, ten bags of heroin were discovered inside the torn lining of his basketball jacket. He was obviously an addict dealing in junk.

An addict who was not a pusher but only making a score for himself might have operated a little differently: Almost invariably when an addict makes a connection any distance from his own neighborhood, he stuffs the heroin into a balloon. He holds the balloon in his hand when he hits the street. If he spots the "Man," he tosses the balloon into his mouth and swallows it. When the police search him, he's clean. And as soon as he's in some quiet place, he sticks his fingers down his throat and vomits. The rubber balloon has protected the heroin and he's got instant paradise for another few hours.

Down at the police station I went over to talk with the boy after he'd been booked. His name was Louie. He was sitting crouched over the edge of his chair, wringing his hands and looking at the floor.

"Man, this is the second time I'm busted."

"Are you scared?"

"Damn right I'm scared. I'm gonna' need a fix! I was about to 'hit the cooker' [take a shot] when you guys came along."

"How old are you?"

"Twenty-two."

"Are you from Manhattan?"

He shook his head. "Queens."

"Do you still live there?"

He nodded. "Not at home, though. Too wild a scene. Split about a year ago."

"Where do you live now?"

"Anywhere, everywhere," he shrugged. "Sometimes I get enough bread pushing junk to get a rathole room somewhere. But mostly I crash wherever someone lets me."

I asked him about his family.

"My old man's a doctor. A GP. Wanted me to be one, too." For the first time since I'd started talking with him he raised his head and looked at me. "He was always talking about us being a father-and-son team." He paused, "Ya' know, I can even remember when I used to get excited about it!" He shook his head slowly, "Man, that was another life ago." He turned his head away and looked back down at the floor.

One of the detectives came over with a couple of Cokes.

Louie drank his down in one gulp. I handed him mine, but he just passed it back and forth in his hands as he continued to talk in a flat, resigned voice: "Man would you believe that four years ago I was a big athlete? Track. Big track star." He shrugged his narrow drooping shoulders. "Yeah, a real long-distance runner. Damn good, too," he added with the most spirit he'd shown since telling me he was scared because he needed a fix. Looking at this pale, skinny, empty-eyed kid it was impossible to believe he'd ever had that kind of endurance. "Real damn good," he muttered under his breath almost as if he, too, found it unbelievable.

"How did you get onto drugs?"

"My buddies. Man, everybody smoked pot. Everyone who counted, anyway. Al and Joey, my two best buddies, kept bugging me to try it. They'd kid me about being the athlete of the century while the real world went by me. They never were impressed when I'd win a meet. And they were my two best buddies. So, one day when track was rained out I said okay. Big deal. Nothing else to do in the rain. So, they take me to a deserted parking lot near school and give me the pot. And, you know, it *was* beautiful! We just rapped for hours." He paused to take a gulp from my Coke bottle. He seemed anxious to keep talking. Compulsive. "So then, Al and Joey, me, and a couple of other guys started smoking together. Like a club. We found this abandoned heap. Great old, sort of red Mercury. It was our clubhouse. Man, we'd roll up those windows and blow our minds. When I smoked pot, the world was rosy. But after I'd get real jittery and upset. Nervous. Felt real cooped up, you know?"

His schoolwork disintegrated. He was off the track team. He was smoking pot continuously and "chipping" (using heroin) occasionally.

"It was great being with my best buddies, but everything

else was a bust. Started falling asleep right in class. My old man really blew his stack when they said I'd have to stay back a year. He hired a tutor, but I fell asleep on him, too. The fights at home were unbelievable." He paused thoughtfully before continuing. "My mother never said anything the whole time. Just moped around like a martyr. She found some blood on my sheets a couple of times, but I said it was from mosquito bites or something. She'd just look at me kinda' funny and walk away." Louie took another mouthful of Coke. "She didn't even cry. Not once. Not even when I was picked up a couple of times for suspected breaking and entry. Never could prove it, though. But she must have known because I was stealing from her, too. From the food envelope and the change on the dresser. What could I do? Al and Joey weren't giving me the stuff anymore. I had to buy it. And it just got worse at home. I dropped out of school after a big brawl with my old man. Man, he ranted and raved about what he did or didn't do as a kid. And what the fuzz or principal would do to me and how I was a rotten influence on little kids. Honest to God, I never sold or gave junk to little kids! Man, I was a real wreck from all these fights. Really, I was just about over the edge. But Al gave me some heroin one day and I started chipping when it was real bad. I'd lock myself in the bathroom and shoot up and it would be okay for a while. But then I'd get depressed and need more. Getting the bread wasn't easy either. Man, it's been a rough year on the pocket for 'snow.' A few times I even went hustling in drag." Louie looked up, shifted his position a few times, and continued. "I was real desperate. I'd dress up like a hooker and hustle late at night when the suckers would be too loaded to pay close attention. I'd take them up to a deserted loft where Al and Joey were waiting and we'd roll 'em," he finished, matter of factly. "But we never hurt them. No rough stuff. Just take their money. I can honestly say we never once hurt anyone."

"Louie, did you ever try to talk with your father about your problems?"

"Sure, he always spoke *to* me, but he never spoke to *me*."

Such a parental reaction may be understandable to me as a priest, but not to this young man. He felt excluded. Everyone else had been injured but him. And paradoxically, he was the one who was really dying.

Some parents when they are catapulted into such a set of circumstances try to deceive themselves with the strange naïveté that this is just a fad with their children. By some vague curative action their children will be incubated against any real evil effects until the fad passes. Rationalizing like this only allows the young person to sink deeper into the quicksand of drug abuse. Letting your hair grow, this is a fad, and kids may resort to a hundred harmless hip things like it. But resorting to mind-eroding, self-destructive drugs, this is addiction or psychological habituation that can lead to addiction. For parents to indulge in such simplistic mutual consolation is utter nonsense. Such self-deception only temporarily banks the tiny volcanoes of anxiety and when the full impact of the dreadful reality bursts upon the scene—that your child is hooked—the eruption will be deafening. The flying sparks usually include threats, warnings, commands, and ultimatums. Then the shattering culmination is reached—namely, a severing of all lines of communication with the young addict or potential addict, and even eviction of him from the home.

Drug abuse is no passing fancy. This is a plague that is killing a generation of saplings. Destroying the timber that ought to be the foundation and future strength of this country. Drugs are cutting the heart out of America. And yet, supercilious people publicly make flip, hedonistic, and careless remarks that can only misinform and prolong this disastrous dilemma. This is also no time for paltry and token monetary donations with consequently inadequate narcotics programs.

Once, Louie was considering a career in medicine. A career as broad and as fascinating as the human mechanism itself. But drugs changed all that. They bound him hard and fast. They restricted his horizons to a glassine bag no bigger than a postage stamp. Mind-expanding? Not on your life. He doesn't know one new thing about medicine. But ask him about that bag. He knows the wonderful feel of it. The softness inside makes his hands tremble with ecstatic delight. He knows the thrill of relief that rattles his brain as he holds it in his hand, caresses it, crushes it to his body; even the crinkling of the paper is music to his ears. Just flat and square and small, yet the mere sight of that bag is one of the wonders of the world. It brings sparkle to dead eyes, chills to a very weak spine. And its possession is a priceless treasure.

We talked for a while longer, and I finally asked,

"Louie, Why do you stay on junk?"

"All I know is the only time I'm not scared is when I'm tight."

I thought to myself, that's really the long and short of it. So many scared people; scared of being blown to bits by the Bomb; scared of choking to death from the filthy air; scared of dying slowly from disease or biological warfare; scared of being the color that God made you; scared that there is no God; scared of the Boss; scared about paying the bills; scared of being yourself; scared of failure; and most of all, scared of love. So many people churning inside. So many people wanting to give and needing to receive, and yet, afraid.

Louie seemed to want to continue the subject of his getting clean. "I think I could this time, if I could get a good start. But man, it's awful scary if you don't have someone to listen and help you."

"Are you ready to accept the responsibility of your decision to kick it?"

"I just know where I'm at now is hell. I guess I'll never be a doctor, but, I'm better than this, man, I'm better than this." He looked at me pleadingly. "I'm ready, but I can't do it alone."

In times past, Louie would have been left to languish in jail without the opportunity of another chance. Now the Narcotic Addict Rehabilitation Act of 1966 makes for a more optimistic future. The provisions of this Act state that any addict who is busted for a nonviolent crime can make it known that he is willing to be committed for treatment and rehabilitation. Subsequent to such a decision by the addict, he or she is committed to the Secretary of Health, Education and Welfare. However, if the addict has already been convicted of some crime, then the addict must, if willing, come under the jurisdiction of the Attorney General. This commitment cannot be for more than ten years or the length of time that would have been served for the conviction. On the other hand, an addict who has not been busted for any crime can voluntarily commit himself or be committed by some relative or friend. Such an Act is a humane step in the right direction. Still, *the* most important part of this whole program is what happens to the ex-addict when he is released from a hospital or rehabilitation center —follow-up rehabilitation is the single necessary factor in accomplishing successful cures after detoxification. Louie's problem, along with many other addicts, was that once released from treatment he'd been sent back to the same environment, the same temptations, the same friends. Any new interest or motivation that had come to him during clinical treatment died as soon as he hit the street.

6

The Pill Age

I have the curious distinction of being the only priest I know who has been in almost every sleazy bar in New York. This does not exactly qualify me for the Communion Breakfast circuit, but in certain circles it does bestow a unique status. The most incredible part about walking into any one of these crummy emporiums is the realization that two doors down the block there is a crummier place. Most of them are euphemistically dubbed "cocktail lounges" or some other absurd misnomer, and my reason for exploring their premises was always connected with Narcotics Squad patroling.

Enormous effort and time is spent patroling the streets. Checking in bars, making a stop at a small candystore, asking a hotel clerk a few questions, talking with the cop on the beat, all of it is calculated to eventually stop the illegal distribution of narcotics. Up and down the shadowy boulevard and in and out of joints you ordinarily wouldn't want to be caught dead in.

Frequenting disreputable places wasn't the full curriculum of my activities with the squad. One day I sat in the stands with two detectives and watched a high-school football team practice. On our end of the field a young high-school senior was practicing kicking extra points. He was good. The ball came end-over-end through the uprights every time. "That young kicker is on probation, Father. We picked him up for illegal possession of pills about eight months ago." He was a husky kid and from a good family. We wandered down onto the field, and I started talking to him. He loved sports, and oddly enough it was through sports that he got turned on to pills. He said quite a few of the members of the football team use them. I asked him what kind of pills he was using before he got caught. "I used to take 'downers' [barbiturates]. You see, I don't get into the game except to kick. With a couple of pills I'm real relaxed and I land soft if somebody hits me. I don't get injured so easy."

The coach went on to relate why the kids were using pills. He said they practice hard every afternoon until about seven P.M. When the kids go home they claim they are too tired to study or go out on a date, so they start taking pills. Some of them take them for the game also. "I used to think some of the kids were really hustlers, really wanted to make the team. They never seemed to get tired. They would scrap for that extra yard and follow that ball all over the field. Then I found out they were on pep pills [amphetamines]. I should have known," he said, "because they would never stop talking on the bench when I took them out of a game. They used to drive me crazy with their constant chatter."

I thought to myself, even sports, which are supposed to be a good healthy outlet, instill a spirit of competition and respect for the other guy; even this domain had been sullied by drug abuse. We disqualify horses if just a trace of a chemical is found in their system after a race, yet, I've read articles in sports magazines that make pill-taking by our best athletes seem as common and as ordinary as running ten laps used to be to get in shape. Once again, young people hearing and reading about this easily follow suit. If it's in the paper, a magazine, or on TV, it must be okay, or, at least, not that bad.

Sports are another instance where a young person has the chance to develop interpersonal maturity by pitting himself fairly against someone else. This necessary opportunity is again destroyed by drugs, which give an advantage the young person really does not possess. Instead of taking pride in his own abilities or learning to humbly respect the prowess of another, the young person is learning to decline and lie to himself. This character-building quality of sports is also impaired by adults who value winning more than a game played to the best of one's ability. This attitude has induced more than one young person to start swallowing pills in order to achieve the all-important winner's laurels. Despite the psychological injury that might be involved here, there is also the very real possibility of physical injury while engaging in sports under the influence of pills. And we haven't even mentioned the worst consequence of all, that of becoming a drug addict.

One day the detectives and I were sitting in a car outside a high school watching a street vendor with one of those small hotdog pushcarts. They suspected him of selling pills to the students. A week later, after this pusher had been busted, we went into this same school and opened three lockers belonging to suspect students. We found three jars of pills. The students sell them among themselves. All colors, all sizes, all "ups" or "downs"—you name it and the average high-school student can most probably buy it right in his school. Or there may be an enterprising student around who gives them away free with the hope of building up a future paying clientele.

This is a bad scene. But it really shouldn't come as too much of a surprise. These young people were born into a pill age.

We created it. We are living in it. Now we must learn to cope with it—before it destroys us!

I place addiction to pills in a different league from heroin—addiction to pills is far worse! It's worse because kids equate addiction only with heroin and the opiates. They think of pill-popping as a new sport. Pills of all types, from vitamins to patent nerve tranquilizers, are so widely advertised, so freely dispensed, and so willingly swallowed by the public that they do not bear the stigma of hard drugs.

"Christmas trees," "drivers," and "footballs"—amusing names that make the pill scene seem like one big game. But the real name of the game is *speed.* Open the hand of any kid who has just bought five pills for ten cents apiece in the high-school locker room or at the neighborhood hotdog stand. You may find, mixed with the barbiturates, a "dexie" or a "bennie." Shocking? Think about it. How long has this been going on?

For over forty years truck drivers have downed a few bennies with their last cup of coffee before they hit the road on long night hauls. People in the glamour business, where competition is savage and deadlines close—pop music . . . TV . . . movies . . . theater . . . sports . . . advertising—have been using some form of "speed" since the 1930s to increase their endurance and ensure a brilliant performance. Hundreds of thousands of medicine cabinets throughout America also contain some form of speed—the public calls them diet pills and prescription cold pills. Doctors, however, know these pills as the useful but potentially dangerous amphetamines: dexedrine and benzedrine.

In junkie argot amphetamines are known as uppers, because they generate tremendous bursts of energy and an exaggerated sense of well-being. Although users generally take speed in pill form, liquid amphetamines can be injected directly into the vein—hence the phrase, "shoot some speed." To reach a high, some pill-poppers may take as many as fifteen to twenty-five uppers of varying chemical content. A high may last several days or a week, depending on the user's finances and his physical endurance: Speed blocks all desire for food and sleep. Coming down from a high is known as "crashing"—the user becomes intensely depressed; his ego seems fragmented; his body, already starved for nourishment and sleep, may be wracked by uncontrollable muscle spasms. To cushion his crash, the seasoned user may shoot heroin or take a mixture of uppers and barbiturates, and the vicious circle of addiction continues.

Police records show that many teen-agers involved in crimes of unusual brutality, street riots, or vandalism have been speeding.

The colorful repertoire of barbiturates, or downers, includes "red birds," "rainbows," "greenies," "tooies," and "reds." Because a teen-ager never knows exactly the type or strength of the pills he is using, he may swallow three or four—some depressants, some stimulants—which will work dangerously against each other. If, in addition, he drinks alcohol, it may kill him.

The fangs of barbiturate addiction sink deep. The young people do not realize how serious it is. Since pills are so freely used and dispensed, they do not have a sinister enigma attached to them. But barbiturates cause serious psychological dependence, physical dependence, and they develop a body-tolerance factor. Like an opiate, the person has to keep taking more and more barbiturates to satisfy his compulsive desires. Unlike opiates, after a while barbiturates attack the nervous system and affect the brain so that a person can become retarded or simple-minded.

In speaking to a group of young girls I once gave the

example that if a person was taking very pure heroin, and at the same time was eating three square meals a day and getting a good night's sleep, the heroin would not have any direct deleterious effect on the body. A young girl, who had that cryptic look a woman has when she thinks she knows something you don't, spoke up and said, "You mean if I was real rich and able to buy good heroin, and I had servants cook me three good meals, and I slept every night, it would be all right to be a drug addict?" I answered, "No." Although the heroin in this case would not directly harm her body, it would indirectly cause irregularities in her life that would eventually destroy her. Witness the many rich and famous people who have destroyed themselves with drugs or alcohol. And whereas heroin does not necessarily attack the body, barbiturates can multilate it.

A person on barbiturates can have the same outward characteristics as a person intoxicated by alcohol. If you try to reason with a person in this state, it is very difficult to communicate. I waited in an apartment-house hallway one night for just such an opportunity. There were no offensive odors in this hallway, no cracking linoleum runners down the center of the floor, and no forty-watt bulb straining to give light. This was strictly uptown, top-drawer merchandise with wall-to-wall luxury. But the sounds coming from Apartment 603A were the same desperate noises you might have heard in the shabbiest tenement. The death-rattle of drug abuse. The detectives knocked on the door with no answer. But the voices became silent; only the music could still be heard. Then the door opened just a crack and the detectives lunged against it, forcing it open all the way. There was some scrambling, but there was no place to go. We were on the sixth floor and one of the detectives had the only door to the apartment blocked. Now the apartment was filled with squeals and sobs, and an occasional "We didn't do nothing."

The kids, all ranging between fourteen and eighteen, were stoned out of their minds on pills. Most of them were so groggy they still had pills on their person. The host of the party was a seventeen-year-old boy. I made an attempt to speak with him, but he was hardly coherent. His parents had taken a weekend trip and left him home alone. They took their fourteen-year-old daughter with them. I was present when the detectives were talking to this father the next day. He said that he thought his son was drinking. "He came home staggering a few times, but I just thought he had had a few beers." If the father had taken time to learn something about narcotics, he would have noticed that even though his son looked drunk there was no smell of alcohol. Maybe if the father, like many fathers, had taken time to learn something about his son, no one would have to know anything about narcotics.

The police will tell you that it is not uncommon to bust up pill parties in the homes or apartments of parents who have gone away and left their teen-agers unsupervised. And this is happening in the more affluent families; the people living in the nice suburbs away from the dirty city. When parents reach the point where their teen-agers are looked upon as cramping their style, they should not underestimate or be surprised at the ability of the youngster to compensate for that rejection. Leaving a teen-ager home alone with too much money and an overabundance of unchecked free time is asking for trouble.

We ran into one case where the teen-ager had enough personal gumption not to take part in a pill party while her parents were away. But being a normal teen-ager she wanted to avoid being on the outs with the gang completely, so she let them use her parents' house. They almost ruined the place. When the parents returned, they didn't know whether to be thankful that their daughter was all right or angry that their house was demolished. They wouldn't have had to make such a decision if they had stayed home or taken their daughter with them in the first place.

Sometimes when the detectives would notify the parents that they had busted a party in their home, or that their son or daughter was involved in such a party, I would get the distinct impression that the parents were annoyed with the police for making the raid. They almost seemed to say, "Well, it's really not that bad, we don't know what you're making all the fuss about." Finding such defensiveness on the part of today's parents is not an isolated phenomenon. The cause for such an attitude may lie in the fact that parents are closer to their children today. Not necessarily in the best sense, but in such a way as to inflict their personality and ambitions so forcefully on the child that any criticism of the young person is taken as a personal jibe at them. Years ago young people for the most part were expected to take their lumps if they did something wrong. The parents backed up the teacher or whatever authority might be involved in making the correction. Today, some parents are more apt to have the teacher put in jail and the authority reprimanded for unjustly picking on their child. Children, of course, because they are young, will take advantage of these situations. But because they also have a terrific sense of justice, they will begin to question the sincerity of adults and eventually lose respect for their parents and for authority in general. Rather than helping the young person, such overprotectiveness imparts a weakness.

Whenever I speak to parents I illustrate this point by relating the following story. It was once told by Dr. Joseph Fort Newton and it concerns a young scientist who was watching a butterfly emerge from its cocoon. The poor butterfly struggled desperately to get free. He wiggled and pulled and squirmed. The pain seemed too great to let it continue, so the young scientist decided to help the butterfly. He felt sorry for it so he took a knife and made the hole at the end of the cocoon a little bigger so that the butterfly could slip out more easily. This action was to teach the scientist a severe lesson. He had ended the butterfly's struggle all right, but when the butterfly emerged from the cocoon it was a cripple. Its wings were misshapen and it couldn't fly. All it could do was flop around on the ground and wait to die. Instead of being a friend to that butterfly, that young scientist had been an enemy.

How often do parents feel the same way about their children? They hate to see them struggle; they don't want to see them hurt; they can't bear to watch them suffer. As a result, they make the same mistake the young scientist made. They step in and decide to shield them from the struggle and pain. The young people never get the opportunity to overcome difficult obstacles. They never know the satisfaction and delight in conquering hardships. Through misguided affection some parents sap the strength of their children and force them to face life weakened and maimed.

The day is long past when parents can raise their children wisely and prudently all by themselves. There are too many outside influences working against the parents. For this reason, when other external authorities offer to help, this aid should not be rejected or immediately branded prejudicial. This is particularly true when it concerns narcotics. Passing off pill consumption as just a youthful lark can be a dangerous mistake.

The inclination to reach for pills in the face of every tension is a growing mania among our youth. A life based on such a pill reflex is a blurred fiasco and a ticket to insanity. I stood in an emergency room once and watched a girl in the agony of barbiturate withdrawal. Her suffering was so great you wondered how there could be any shred of sanity left. I tried to talk to her and her eyes blazed as if her soul was on fire. She weighed only 110 pounds, but she squeezed my hand until I thought every knuckle would break. Pills were supposed to help her escape the world's pain, but there is no escape. Only if we face it each day in small doses can we dilute it by our happier moments. Trying to avoid pain entirely with pills only condemns us to the scourge of having to endure it all at once like this young girl.

Each day we live is a new adventure. And we learn how to handle tomorrow from the day before. But if all our yesterdays are lost in the twilight of pill addiction, then our tomorrows are doomed to be dismal failures. How did Shakespeare put it, "Brave conquerors! For so you are, that war against your own affections and the huge army of the world's desires." Learning to face life under your own steam doesn't take the sting out of it, but it develops a flexible personality and a defense against crushing discouragement. Pill dependence can only hatch a future of frightened weaklings—mentally immature or defective people who are always looking for the easy cop-out. If, according to the young people, love must be the dominant force to save society, then they had better omit pill dependence from the master plan. Love can only grow and mature through conscious pain and struggle to please the beloved. Nothing grows or changes without struggle and effort and pain. Anyone who believes they can drug themselves insensitive to the rest of the world and in this dormant condition somehow miraculously grow along with it, is sadly misguided. This is an infantile philosophy guaranteed to make you a loser.

There are people who use pills not because they reflect any special trend of thought or particular kind of protest, but simply because they get hooked accidentally. This is a very real danger, and it happens more often than we care to admit.

I met one of these people not long ago in the out-patient clinic of a well-known New York hospital. An attractive blond in her mid-twenties and obviously pregnant walked by the nurses' station and asked if she could speak with me in her room when I was free. When I got back to the woman's room she was sitting on the edge of the bed. She said she had signed herself in that morning for gynecologic reasons, but tomorrow she was going to tell the doctor the real reason. She was taking barbiturates and she couldn't stop. Her baby was due in two more months, and all she was worrying about was pills. She had already fallen twice and was afraid she was going to injure the child. I listened to her words, which were well-moistened with tears. Then she asked me the big question. "Father, can you get me some pills until the doctor comes tomorrow morning?" "Why don't you tell the doctor the truth now, so they can give you something? I can't get you anything," I said. Now she was begging and pleading. I left the room and went to the nurses' station.

I inquired about the woman's doctor and asked the nurse if she would inform him concerning the problem. The nurse said she would call immediately, and I went back to the room. The woman was sobbing with deep gasps. She seemed on the brink of despair. I told her I had taken the liberty to have her doctor informed and that I was sure he would order some sedation soon. She looked at me and I could detect the hurt in her eyes. She was wiping her eyes with a handkerchief now, and I spoke to her about the baby. She never said another word. She just sat there blankly. I gave her my blessing and promised to stop in that evening.

About nine o'clock that night, I stopped at the door of this woman's room and it was empty. I went to the nurses' desk and asked where she was. The nurse replied that she had checked herself out that afternoon. My heart sank. She had signed herself in out of desperation, but she had never really decided to stay.

She was not the first pregnant woman to get hooked on pills. With all the various sicknesses during pregnancy, doctors often prescribe pills to be taken as directed. Some women start taking more than they should on particularly rough days. Before long the steel grip of pill dependence has them by the throat. Another unfortunate accident involved in all this is the fact that when the baby is born, it will be born addicted and will have to go through withdrawal symptoms. No plague from outer space could spread more devastation than our drug-abuse problem. And pills, as innocent and familiar as they seem, are a major culprit in this massive slavery.

7

Caution—"Mind"-Field

No special physical requirements or talents are needed to qualify as a professional addict. If you start off slowly with the cool stuff, all you need is a good set of veins that can be punctured, pierced, stabbed, needled, and lacerated, and a throat that can swallow anything from "goofers" and downers to Christmas trees and "meth"—all calculated to produce either a groggy dolt or a hyperactive screwball. Correction: You may have to practice swallowing small plastic bags of junk or balloons of marijuana—just in case of a sudden raid.

You think there is still time. Meanwhile, you're just planning to experiment a little—blowing, chipping, dropping, joy-popping—until the right career suddenly occurs to you! Don't worry about it anymore, man! You're already doing your thing! If you don't think drug abuse is a total vocation, the next time you talk to a strung-out junkie or an acidhead ask him (or her) what else he's been doing lately—besides stealing, whoring, or pushing in order to get that fix.

Postwar society's increasingly frequent and often inaccurate discussion of drug use has almost totally stripped addiction of the sinister horror it held for the previous generation. But even today's more tolerant attitudes toward drugs have not been able to totally erase the traditional concepts of drug use and abuse that many parents still hold: concepts that cause them to react with outraged dignity, blind anger, or physical violence, in addition to turning their home into a jail. Under these conditions it should not surprise anyone when the teenager's attitude is: "As long as they treat me like an addict, I might as well be one!" Certainly an immature reaction, but a very possible one—especially when he considers himself "merely experimenting."

When parents discover their child is experimenting with drugs, they can best assist him by being as approachable as possible. In this context, pointing out the potential dangers of drugs with the hope of arousing sensible and healthy fears, is not psychologically damaging. Obviously, fear should not be the basic reason for avoiding drugs, but at the same time, parents would be foolhardy not to value reasonable fear as a useful tool in their campaign. It is prudent fear of pain that keeps us from walking in front of cars, or sticking our hand in a fire. Presumably then, to live a reasonable and happy life a reasonable and prudent fear should be part of our emotional makeup. However, parents must remember that teen-agers rarely consider potential danger, and therefore do not fear its consequences.

In the midst of the well-advertised superabundance of the "Plastic Age" we are living in a spiritual and religious famine. Stuffed-shirt society in its false sophistication has forgotten that God is instantly accessible through prayer. Prayer, that beautiful act of lifting up your mind and heart to Him wherever you happen to be—at the office, in your kitchen, in study hall, digging a ditch, driving a bus. Twentieth-century man, with his genius for neat prefabrication and prepackaging, has neatly prepackaged God in a rigid, airless, formal box marked "Do not open until Sunday." The other six days man acts, works, and lives as if he alone were running the world.

Our advanced science and technology offer young people many shiny, disposable delights and promise even more wonders to come—utopia, here and now! The older generation cannot see what empty promises these are, for a very valid reason—aside from the essential professions of medicine, law, the ministry, food production, and so on, most of the jobs in the world today are involved directly with the production, promotion, and sale of pushbutton happiness. They are too involved with making a buck in order to keep up the payments on the mortgage, the second car, the color TV, last year's vacation—all the so-called advantages a man can give his wife and kids. They are just too tired from the dull, dehumanized, brutal daily grind of "business as usual." They are too brainwashed and pacified by the false liturgy of materialism composed by the high priests of the advertising and public-relations media. They have been chained to this treadmill too long to stand back and see that they are rapidly going nowhere.

Even the social scientists believe that all the ills of society, most importantly drug abuse, stem directly from the lack of these material advantages. Politicians, quick to capitalize on these quasi-official pronouncements for the sake of votes, vote more and more money for empty giveaway programs to lull the poor into a false sense of well-being. Society never offers God as part of the utopian "care package." Instead, He has been supplanted by slogans for positive thinking, native ability, good medicine, and Lady Luck. Curiously enough, these quaint replacements hint at a power beyond human knowledge.

Make no mistake about it, everybody wants to be saved—from something! From war, from poverty, from ignorance, from disease, from job insecurity, from crab grass in the lawn. It's a comfortable religion, at once too abstract and too trivial to hit at the guts of a man's conscience. Is the only business of religion today so-called social reform? Is this the rough, demanding road to personal spiritual fulfillment, or just the same old garden path to our plastic utopia?

Youth today has the luxury of time and the unspoiled idealism to examine our society with a critical eye. They are intelligent, idealistic, and generous, and they long for commitment to a truly great idea or cause. Their whole being cries out that the products of technology are not enough. . . . There must be more to life than that! They refuse to have their lives computerized. Spiritually unarmed, they stand in the throes of rebellion against the empty materialism of a world they never made. Pitifully ignorant of the fulfillment and excitement of a truly God-centered life, these teen-agers have mistakenly turned to the mind-bending drugs to help them reach out beyond themselves.

Hallucinogenic drugs are being touted as having charismatic qualities, talent-scout abilities, and spiritual dynamism. Entire cults have been formed around the core of narcotics and their so-called mystical, mind-expanding properties. The God they see in their psychedelic visions is a manufactured fake, a trumped-up mystical figment of their drugged and deluded minds.

The whole psychedelic scene grooves on the supernatural. Kids will gyrate to the blown apart and out-of-sight pulsations of acid-rock, achieving a certain refuge and fleeting insensibility from the battering and punching sounds. But the lasting and intense interchange they unconsciously seek can come only from the touch of the Master's hand. God may have to wear a million different hats and assume as many different images before the psychedelic generation finds and appreciates Him for what He is in Himself. Karl Marx once wrote that "Religion is the opiate of the masses." If we allow the drug scene to flourish, it will be written of our society that "Opiates are the religion of the masses."

One night I received a phone call from an acquaintance who knew I was traveling with the Narcotics Squad. He sounded excited and his words were so garbled with emotion I could scarcely understand him. I asked him to calm down and repeat what he had just said. He was calling from the house of a young couple, Brian and Shirley, who lived next door to him. The wife had taken some powerful drug and she had a gun. . . . She was threatening to kill herself. . . . No one could take the gun away from her. This last remark sent a few shivers up my spine. I told him to call a doctor and the police and that I would be right over.

Ironically, when I received the call there was a young engaged couple in my office to whom I was giving the usual course of premarital instructions. The situation was typical of the gamut of situations the priest must face in a given day. In one instant, I was dealing with a young couple who were looking toward the future with brimming optimism and lighthearted courage. They were eager to face life and conquer it. In the next, I was involved with a young couple whose future looked dismal and bleak. A husband filled with worry and consternation and a wife with insane thoughts of self-destruction. I explained to the couple before me the reason for my impromptu exit and rushed out to the car.

The house was only fifteen minutes away, but this can be an eternity when a person's life is at stake. I drove as fast as I could; just short of being reckless. I was hoping that the police would stop me. I was sure if they knew why I was hurrying they would escort me the rest of the way. The idea of the gun kept popping into my mind. I had heard stories about people trying to commit suicide and I had read some vivid accounts. But little did I realize that I was riding into a situation very similar to one I had heard related by another priest. I remembered shifting uneasily as I listened to him tell it. I also recalled how grateful I was that it had never happened to me.

When I got to the house the police had already arrived. My friend met me and took me around to the back door. "She's in the front room, Father. We better go through the kitchen." I tried to get some hurried information, but he said I had better talk to her husband. Two policemen and Brian, the young husband, were in the kitchen. The doctor had not arrived yet, but he was on his way. I shook hands with Brian, who looked to be about nineteen or twenty years old. He had long hair and a scruffy, uneven beard. I asked him about his wife. "She must be on a bad trip. She won't let me near her. She's been all hung-up with this spirit cult, I mean, whacked out!" he said. I asked where she was, and one of the policemen pointed into the next room.

When I walked into the living room and saw her I could almost feel every pore in my body open up in cold sweat. She was sitting motionless in a chair with the barrel of a pistol clenched tightly between her teeth. I felt my Roman collar press hard against my throat as I tried to swallow my fear. My mind roared with static and my tongue felt thick and useless. I moved slowly onto the edge of an armchair, but never once took my eyes off her. The gun looked so big in her tiny hand. She was wearing a pair of pajamas and her eyes stared right past me. What was going on in her mind? She made no sign to acknowledge my presence. One false move could make her pull that trigger and blow off the back of her head. What would she consider a false move? I was also starkly aware that at any moment she might take the gun out of her mouth and train it on me. I felt my stomach turn completely over and settle uncertainly. I heard the sound of my own pulse in my neck booming in my ears as I searched wildly for the right phrases. How many times had I seen situations similar to this in the movies or on TV where the eloquence of the person trying to help held me spellbound—I was sick and dumb.

After what seemed a long time, I started to speak. My voice sounded so far away, like a bad tape recording. It wasn't even me. It was as if I was watching her and someone else was doing the talking. And believe me, I watched her every second. I heard the kitchen door open and someone said the word "Doctor." I was glad he had arrived, but hoped he wouldn't walk in the room while I was talking to Shirley. At this point any sudden interruption or surprise could be fatal. I spoke in the softest tones I could muster, all the while praying for the wisdom to say the right thing. I was afraid the very sound of my words might startle her or suggest some radical type of action. At one point I said, "Now you really don't want to kill yourself," and I bit my tongue when I said the word "kill." Shirley never moved a muscle and I kept right on rambling. To this day I don't remember half of what I said.

One thing I do remember with tremendous relief. It remains in my mind, graphic and undimmed. After about an hour of my picking my way through a verbal minefield, without warning, Shirley slowly and carefully took the pistol out of her mouth and laid it on the floor beside her chair. Not altering my tone as I continued to talk, I wondered if I would be able to get to the gun before she could pick it up again. Then suddenly she slumped back into the chair like a collapsing puppet. I quickly grabbed the gun and yelled for the doctor to come in. She struggled a little bit as the doctor examined her. He couldn't prescribe anything for her until he found out exactly what she had taken. The doctor wanted her in the hospital immediately for lab tests and a few days of observation. The police checked the automatic pistol and said there were two bullets in it, but they were not in the firing chamber and she would have had to pull the trigger twice before the first one was fired—at that particular moment that piece of information was of little or no consolation to me! It was summer and I had perspired right through my suit. I was wilted and wet, but tremendously relieved.

Shirley was whimpering like a little child now, and she refused to let her mother take her into the bedroom to get dressed. The mother had arrived about the same time as the doctor. With a pouting expression she said she didn't want to get dressed and that she wasn't going to ride in any old ambulance. When the doctor suggested that Brian drive her to the hospital, she cried, and said she wouldn't go unless I came with her. I assured her I would. He helped her into a robe and we started to walk out to the car very slowly.

The mother began to lash out at Brian. She said he was nothing but a dirty hippie and if it wasn't for his marijuana smoking, her daughter would never have started on drugs. I tried to calm her with the warning that continuing the argument would upset her daughter—we could talk it out later. I need not have worried; Shirley was really out of it. I am sure she was not fully aware of anything that was going on around her. The ride to the hospital was uneventful. She sat quietly making faces and dribbling out of the corners of her mouth. Every once in a while she mumbled a few garbled words and phrases.

Shirley had "dropped some acid" (taken LSD). When I spoke to her a week later in the psychiatric ward, she did not remember a single thing that had happened. The LSD trip had upset the delicate balance of her mental stability. I'm sure I seemed just another part of her trip. Maybe my words that day sounded like clanging bells. Maybe I looked like a giant toad filled with noisy colors. Whatever went on in that poor girl's mind, though, thank God, did not amount to a final trip for either of us.

Shirley, at eighteen, was a budding artist going to a nearby college. She longed for spiritual insights. She wanted to get deep inside herself and scoop up handfuls of her own identity. Mystical leaps into the hidden places of her own being had convinced her that she had spoken to God.

When this young wife first started college, she was prepared to experience self-relevation the pick-and-shovel way through everyday living. This plan was changed when she came under the influence of a classmate who manufactured his own acid—he used it as a crutch to build up his own ego and to stimulate his artistic talent. Most probably his artistic talent was half-baked before LSD and remained just as impoverished after LSD! Nevertheless, his claims of esthetic and religious exploration hooked her into a small circle of cultists. It is one of the unfortunate realities of our society that the truly creative, sincere, and talented people of society do not talk about God, religion, and spirituality as freely as the acidheads.

I have heard addicts counseled—by professionals in their field—as though they were not human beings of flesh, bone, and soul, but more as if they were loosely knitted sweaters with a few dropped stitches. The human spirit can not be unraveled and reknit at will by man alone. Only God can do this. The needs of both body and spirit must be considered if we are to successfully motivate addicts to get "clean" (off drugs) and stay clean. Counseling addicts without mentioning God and his relationship to the whole person is like trying to discuss the Pietà without mentioning Michaelangelo. Yet, today when anyone mentions God during the rehabilitation of addicts, he is immediately accused of violating the First Amendment or trying to force religion down the throat of the hapless addict. The modern trend seems to be to keep God out of "real life"—disinfected and dismissed from His vital role as eternal Creator of all life, he is enshrined in beautiful museums or left forgotten under a glass dome in the attics of men's minds. Only when the generation that is the Establishment fully accepts the challenge of God—the challenge of personal responsibility—the challenge of truth—will the teen-ager turn from the acid solutions to His quest.

8

Greenwich Village Nightclub

Saturday evening, March 22, 1970, I was cruising lower Harlem with two narcotics detectives, looking for a runaway fourteen-year-old addict. It was the kind of relentless, monotonous, and unglamorous work that produces most of the success in police investigations. Our fruitless search through abandoned, garbage-filled tenements was interrupted by a call on the radio to proceed to a nightclub in Greenwich Village. Several undercover informants had reported that a new drink was being sold to "the Pepsi Generation"—cola spiked with acid.

The thought of anybody giving LSD to unsuspecting youngsters was unthinkable. But this is the sort of madness that confronts you on the drug scene. Human beings playing deadly games with the lives of others. Unprincipled scoundrels taking advantage of the hapless young person who thinks he has nothing to fear or knows all there is to know about the drug scene.

The two detectives I was working with this particular evening were young, intelligent, and black. As we got out of the car about a block from the nightspot, one of them jokingly said, "We won't have to worry about a gray cat like you burning our cover in this place, Father; it's all black and white."

We pushed past a long waiting line through the front door and were immediately stopped by two men standing next to a young girl taking tickets. The detectives flashed their identification and asked to see the manager. We stood there for a few minutes waiting and watched the steady stream of young people flood the place.

When the manager arrived he took us to an office off to the side that was actually an old freight elevator converted into a small workroom. The manager was a young man in very mod dress with hair to his shoulders and a full beard. He seemed unusually calm and confident in the presence of the detectives, as if he had gone through this routine many times before.

The walls of the office had about fifteen pictures of large single eyeballs. It was sort of a spooky decor, perhaps symbolic of an external conscience in lieu of any functional internal one. My eyes caught sight of a sign on the desk that seemed to dispute the whole current of permissiveness, of doing your own thing, of the let-it-all-hang-out philosophy that this section of New York and this particular nightspot were trying so desperately to project. It was a simple sign next to two telephones that read, "Do not move these phones from this position, leave them exactly where they are." It was the only indication of reality in the entire room. When you get right down to living and not just dreaming, there must always be some rules and regulations.

The detectives told the manager that we were just going to look around and that as far as he was concerned we weren't even there. He nodded in agreement and we left the office. We headed up the circular ramp leading into the main dancehall. The thunderous beat of the music kept getting louder and louder. Kids were rushing by, some of them no more than ten or twelve years old. The walls and ceilings were covered with psychedelic images of men and women assuming erotic positions. Just looking at the walls gave you the feeling you were on an LSD trip.

When we stepped into the main dancehall, it was pitch-dark. Every now and then psychedelic effects would flash around the walls, but other than that it was total darkness. The kids were packed in like sardines, and the music was incredibly loud. There was no possibility of talking while the band was playing. I couldn't get over how young some of the kids were, and I wondered if their parents even knew they were here.

After my eyes got more accustomed to the darkness I could see couples sitting or standing all along the wall. Many of them were in various stages of stimulated love-making—heavy petting. The music was continuous, and the figures danced in hypnotic rhythm to the blaring cadence. A detective leaned over and shouted in my ear, "Father, let's go over to the soft-drink counter and make our buy." We started across the dance floor with the detective about two steps ahead of me. Halfway across the floor a young man in one of those wide Bonnie-and-Clyde caps stopped the detective. I couldn't hear what they were saying, so I walked over to a narrow hallway leading to the men's room and waited until they were through. After a few minutes the detective came toward me making his way through the crowd. "I just bought three bags of heroin, Father. We're going to collar this guy. When we make our move you follow in after us." Then the detective disappeared up a flight of stairs to my left. Things were beginning to happen, and I felt a little uneasy standing in this place by myself. I moved in closer to the wall and waited.

Acid, horse, speed, probably anything you wanted was right on that dance floor somewhere. Not everybody out there was interested in dancing. The incident that just happened proved the crowd was salted with unsavory and unscrupulous characters. How many kids out there were aware of what was going on around them? They might have a vague notion that there was a possibility of getting drugs in the place. But would they be able to handle the situation if a pusher actually approached them? Would they be able to say "No" if their friends were saying "Yes"? Suddenly finding yourself in a position you had not planned on can make you do things you might be sorry for later.

The sweat was rolling down my face. So many people and no windows turned the place into an oven. As I watched the shadowy figures I thought of all the teen-agers that weren't there. They were probably angry with their parents for saying they couldn't go and had stormed out of the room shouting, "You don't trust me!" How many times have parents heard that reproach? And bringing it down to cases you find it is not a question of trust at all. It is a case of an older and more experienced person foreseeing the possibilities of a trustful young person being taken advantage of. Most parents have complete trust in their children when the situation is in some way commensurate with their experience and maturity. But junkies and pushers a young person meets in this dancehall are slick and devious, wise in the ways of the world, and out to con them at every opportunity.

I saw the two detectives coming down the stairs. They moved right past me and zeroed in on the pusher who had sold us the three bags. The detectives led him off quietly to a side room under the pretense of wanting to buy more heroin. I followed right after them. The room was small and contained a large circular loveseat. The three couples on the loveseat were occupied in expanding their awareness of each other. One of the detectives told them to leave and they straggled out reluctantly, curious as to what was happening.

The entire bust was done as quietly and quickly as possible. The one thing we did not want to do was attract attention. But word had gotten out that something was going on, and a crowd started to gather at the door to the room. One of the detectives went to the door, held up his badge and identification, and said, "Police officers, everyone step back, please." And that's when it started. The crowd began to mutter and rumble. People began shouting "Pig," "Pig!" They were changing from a bewildered, curious crowd to an angry, hostile mob. The pusher had become a martyr.

"Up against the wall, Fascist pigs!" "Get the hell out of here!"

I looked around the room for another door. There was no way out except through the snarling mob. The shouting rose ominously in a steady chant. The two detectives calmly stood in front of the door, both of them holding their badges so the crowd could see, shouting, "Police officers, coming through, please." Suddenly the ugly mob burst through the door forcing the three of us and the pusher against the back wall. Quickly placing the handcuffed pusher and myself behind them, the detectives drew their guns.

"Everybody stand back, police officers coming through!" And still the mob surged toward us, spitting obscenities, undaunted by the sight of guns. The detectives now had no choice—one of them fired a warning shot into the ceiling. It was like a lightning bolt. Everybody scattered. One of the detectives yelled, "Come on, Father!" We burst through the doorway temporarily vacated by the stunned mob and made our getaway.

When we reached the sidewalk we ran down the block to where the car was parked. We were sweating, puffing, and all very grateful to have gotten out of that place unscathed. We never did accomplish our initial purpose for going to that nightspot—namely, to check their soft drinks for LSD. But being sidetracked by unforeseen events is normal for a detective on the Narcotics Squad. Someone else not known would have to go back and continue that investigation. Our cover was burned. But at least this bust would tighten things up for a while.

As we drove to the precinct the detectives questioned the pusher with little success. He was tall, lean, and cool with that choirboy look that could disarm all but these experienced narcs. He emphatically denied selling junk to teen-agers. In fact, the whole bust was one horrible mistake! Then the senior detective asked him the big question: "Man, were the three bags you sold me 'tastin' stuff' [real heroin] or 'beat bags' [dummy bags of sugar or malt]?" The pusher yawned contemptuously in the detective's face.

"Beat bags, man."

Beat bags meant he would be a free man after the report came back negative from the police lab.

The subject of beat bags brings up a very sad point. Pushers like the one above look for what they call "towners" or "weekend hippies." Young people who want to make the scene, blow their mind for a few days, but return to the straight scene for the rest of the week. These pushers sell these inexperienced and anxious kids beat bags. And to illustrate the large role our psyche plays in drug addiction, these kids shoot up nothing but malt sugar and get a real psychological high, as if they were shooting up real heroin. Because they believe they are shooting junk, they get the high. The tragic conclusion to this is that one of these young people is very apt to run into a pusher who will sell him real heroin. Maybe the kid has been shooting up three beat bags, but now, unknown to him, he has three tastin' bags, each with two grains of heroin. Faithful to his previous routine he "hits" with the three bags and winds up dead from an overdose. This is why we are hearing about so many O.D.'s in the past few months. The streets are flooded with beat bags. Another example of how a kid who thinks he can take care of himself can be fatally fooled.

When we reached the precinct, it was alive with activity. Some other detectives had just busted a bar and confiscated a load of cocaine. They had six suspects in the corner cage waiting to be put through the process. We brought our prisoner into one of the side offices and the detectives took the cuffs off him and told him to strip. The young man took off his sweater, shirt, and T-shirt. One of the detectives looked at him and said, "Come on, man, everything, bare-assed naked." When he had taken off the rest of his clothes, the detective said, "Okay, turn around, bend over, and spread your cheeks." This is done to make sure that no bags of heroin are stashed in the rectum. Once again it sounds bizarre, but nothing is unique or beyond trying in an addict's effort to save his junk. The detectives checked his shoes, socks, and every stitch of clothing for concealed dope. When they emptied his pockets on the desk they found a large pushbutton switchblade knife. The detective pushed the button, but the blade didn't open. He looked up at the pusher and said with a smile in his voice, "You don't do anything right, do you? First you sell junk to a policeman, and now your knife doesn't even work."

Monday morning one of the detectives phoned me from the precinct.

"Hey, Father, did you read the paper today?" I said I hadn't.

"Well, they blew up that nightclub about eleven-thirty last night. A lead-pipe timebomb filled with .32 and .38 caliber bullets exploded under the mirrored band platform. Those cats were sprayed with wood, steel, and glass slivers. Seventeen people were taken to a hospital."

A couple of phrases I had thought about the night before popped into my mind—you don't trust me—nothing will happen—I can take care of myself. I wondered how many of the kids who were injured said something like that to their parents just before they went to that crazy place?

9
Misery Revisited

One hot afternoon as we cruised the East Village and spoke regretfully about the young pusher we had just arrested, and about the narcotics problem in general, one of the detectives asked me if I had ever seen a "shooting gallery." The only shooting galleries I knew of were the ones that used to drain my pockets at Coney Island and on the boardwalk at the Jersey shore. Conclusive evidence that another type existed was about to be presented.

We stopped two houses from the corner. The detectives pointed to the third floor and said they had just busted a shooting gallery there the day before. It was only an empty flat now, but he thought I might be curious to see what it looked like. The house had one of those front doors where you have to wait for the buzzer to open it. We rang the superintendent's bell and waited. After a few moments the door was opened cautiously by a shabbily dressed woman of about sixty. Recognizing the detectives, she became hostile and made it very clear she didn't want us to come in, even though she had no choice.

We started up the stairs. The hallway was vacant and

silent. When we were halfway up the steps leading to the third floor, all hell broke loose. We had unsuspectingly walked right smack into the middle of another shooting gallery.

The two detectives moved like lightning trying to grab people before they could clean themselves of dope. Doors were opening and slamming. Men and women stripped to the waist were running into this room and out another. I was standing at the head of the stairs, absolutely frozen by the wild rush of confusion. I noticed a door down the hall in front of me open slightly. Then suddenly it swung wide, crashing off the wall. A man charged out. He was headed for the stairs, right for me. My heart was pounding. My hands were clammy, When he was right in front of me, he veered off into a side room, while ripping off a leather belt he had tied around his arm to pop his veins. The belt flew through the air. Before I could duck, its heavy metal buckle struck me savagely just below my right eye.

Then I saw a woman in her underpants flushing what looked like teabags down the toilet. Desperately she stuffed something into her mouth, but before she could swallow it a detective pried it out with his finger.

The addicts had never expected the detectives to come back to the same place the very next day. They undoubtedly figured the safest place was a flat just busted. The whirlwind activity our appearance generated was not any attempt at violence or escape. It was a frantic effort to get rid of the dope. Eat it, flush it, throw it out the window, but don't get caught with it. An addict will tell you that an average person can leave the house and not give a thought as to what he has in his pockets. But addiction makes even a small thing like that a gigantic and constant worry. One careless, forgetful moment and you may be picked up with heroin dust in your pocket, a forgotten joint in the lining of your coat. The freedom and peace that dope is supposed to impart is a fraud and a sham even in this most simple consideration. The most casual and ordinary movements in everyday life become fraught with dangers and anxiety.

The melee of frightened voices and slamming doors was beginning to subside. The detectives had everybody sitting on the floor against the wall in the outside hallway. There were eleven people in all, three women and eight men—sweaty bodies, some with blood still oozing from the needle punctures, all of them breathing heavily and staring at nothing, through vacant eyes.

Now I knew what a shooting gallery was. A secluded place where psychological cripples shoot dope. They sit around, each one shooting his own favorite dreams or pet delusions into his veins. The tensions, the people who hurt, the world that doesn't care disappears. There is no real communication with each other, no meaningful dialogue, just robotlike beings relinquishing everything that gives them dignity, nobility, and greatness.

The ceremony that accomplishes this distortion of people is a grisly one. They tie off the upper part of the arm with a belt or woman's stocking and make their veins balloon into view. Then they spear into that plump and pulsating vein a hypo filled with heroin that has been dissolved in a little bit of water. The red blood leaks into the hypo and colors the fluid. The binder is ripped off the arm and the body is allowed to suck and play with that needle, until they plunge it home with a swoosh that seems to collapse everything inside with a breathless deathlike sensation. The euphoric stupor that follows is the sweet refuge that keeps the junkie coming back for more at any cost.

Some of their bodies were pretty well shot out, others, it appeared, were just hitting one or two places. The detectives showed me some matchbook covers folded up into tiny triangles. This indicates snorting. A little bit of heroin is emptied into the shovel-like fold. The addict sticks this up his nose and sniffs. An untrained eye looking through a wastebasket would never even notice these matchbooks.

I started wandering from room to room. The glassy-eyed addicts were docile now, waiting their turn to talk to each detective. The decorations in all the rooms were eye-catching, to say the least. Each wall was literally papered from floor to ceiling with pornographic pictures of every conceivable perversion. The flat was rented by one of the girls, Marlene, and she later told me the pictures were her contribution to the world of art. Then, as if to shift the blame—and I almost detected a surprising flush of embarrassment—she said the men liked them when she brought them up to turn a trick. One small room off the kitchen did not have a door, only a long, red plastic drape. I pulled it aside and stepped into a small room. Directly in front of me was a picture of the Virgin Mary almost eight feet tall. In front of the picture were at least twenty-five burning vigil lights. Not small ones, but the tall ones you see in a church. The combination of the hot day and all those burning candles in that small room made it feel like an incubator. The sweat was pouring off me as I stood there in amazement.

One of the detectives walked in and said, "I forgot to mention that we saw the altar here yesterday, Father. I suppose it shouldn't, but it gives me a spooky feeling." I called Marlene in and acted as if I didn't understand anything about Our Blessed Mother. Unabashedly, she explained that this was God's Mother and that she prayed to her to help her make a lot of money when she went out on the streets to hustle as a prostitute. I am certain the Blessed Virgin has had some weird requests from her children here on earth, but none as unusual as this. She seemed completely sincere. Her life and thinking was so distorted by drugs, there was no reason why her sense of religion should not have been twisted also.

The detectives were busy trying to get the addicts to tell

them where the narcotics had come from. The flat alone yielded approximately twelve bags of heroin, three sets of works, some cocaine, and about twenty-four joints.

As I looked at these eleven glassy-eyed, whimpering, dazed people, I wished that every teen-ager in the country who was just about to "experiment" with drugs was there with me. Then they would see for themselves what I saw time after time: No one was smiling. No one was happy. No one was free.

10

Girl Talk

He gave me a patronizing look and said, "Man, don't ask me 'How long?' like there was time for living. Just say, 'When did you die, baby?'" He was nineteen. He was killing time in a cafeteria waiting for a connection. He was a junkie.

It was a cool evening early in October. As we drove through a Brooklyn neighborhood noted for its heavy drug trade, the detectives asked me if I wanted to talk with some addicts in their own scene. A self-service cafeteria well-known to users and pushers was located just two blocks away. Why a cafeteria? The detective explained that most self-service cafeterias provide large shakers of sugar on each table. An addict can delay the onset of withdrawal symptoms by consuming large doses of sugar mixed with his coffee. And sipping a cup of coffee in a public cafeteria makes a perfect cover for the addict as he waits for his connection.

We parked the car on a side street, and as we walked, the detectives commented on the neighborhood. Many of the people we passed were addicts: neatly dressed and well-groomed men and women I would never have suspected as having been busted on narcotics raps. Dressing straight gives the seasoned user the disguise he needs to deal openly in the street, the subway, or in a store.

"See that skinny bald guy in the lumberjacket and khakis coming out of the deli? He works as a hash-slinger at an all-night diner—we busted him twice last year for slinging hash all right—hashish!

"And there's Liz!" He pointed to a fading redhead in a green-and-black print dress.

"She's an ex-hooker—busted once four years ago for possession of cocaine, once for heroin. The plain-looking dark girl with the ponytail going into that beauty shop . . . just got out of Women's Detention House two weeks ago. She was pushing cocaine and pills outside the high school in this district."

Pausing outside the cafeteria, one of the detectives warned me, "Most of the junkies can spot the Man a mile away, Father, so don't expect a welcoming committee." As we pushed through the revolving door and started for a table, I sensed that the air had suddenly become supercharged with tension: feet shuffled nervously under tables; furtive looks passed from group to group; and a cautious murmur eddied through the room—junkie counterintelligence was in high gear. Cups rattled as people pushed back plates full of half-eaten food and prepared to leave. Several junkies known to the detectives walked out slowly, trying to act as nonchalant as possible—unwilling to offend the narcs and risk a bust.

The detectives took a table close to the front door and were soon in deep conversation. Under the guise of collecting material for an article on drug addiction, I began to roam from table to table, talking with the addicts they had pointed out to me.

Almost an hour went by as I hopscotched my way

around the room, but it passed like five minutes. Normally, I find it very uncomfortable to walk up cold to a group and start talking, but this night I was really involved, unmindful of any distracting emotion. This was an abandoned congregation. No priest in any spired cathedral ever felt more relevant than I felt that night. No missionary had souls more starved for the love of God. Here was a Molokai right in the middle of New York. These were outcasts in a dirty marketplace. Didn't Christ go where the smell of fish was strong, the hot odor of sweat smothering, the hair long and dirty? He preached a gospel of love especially to those that the world said were unlovable—the sinners, the weak, the lonely.

Sage advice is not what these souls needed that night, just someone willing to listen. They sat before me broken in body and spirit, yet, in a sense, they were the teachers, they were the wise men. Their tongues were coated with bitterness, rejection, and infantile spite. They taught a cop-out theology, which one day they would grow to hate if ever this demon that charred their brains could be destroyed.

My assigned task as Spiritual Director of the Missionary Cenacle Apostolate was important work, and fulfilling at the same time. Still, the pervasive urgency of this situation made me wonder about the seemingly wasted hours I had spent dickering over tiny changes in the liturgy with some outraged parishioner close to apostacy. The million-and-one inane complaints that had forced me to be consoler and explainer flashed in my memory as so much lamentable drivel; people in good faith manufacturing problems when they really had none. In the presence of these poor, groping young people hanging on to life by a single thread, so much of it seemed foolish. I felt I acquired more rapport with addicts in that one evening than I could have in a whole month of narcotic seminars.

I was just about to call it a night, when an attractive girl with long blond hair stormed through the revolving door followed by a thin, seamy-faced man in his late forties. As they headed for a table in the back, I began to notice odd and incongruous details in their dress and behavior.

The girl was very casually but expensively dressed in a red plaid miniskirt, black suede jacket, and matching black boots—yet she wore dressy white gloves. She seemed angry, and she treated the man beside her with scorn and indifference. He moved as though he was sleepwalking: His jaw hung slack and his eyes rolled out of focus. Each time he wavered toward a table or chair in his path, the girl impatiently snatched at his coat sleeve, as if she couldn't bear to touch his arm. When they reached the last table, she shoved him into a chair, then, hunching her shoulders and jamming her hands into her pockets, she sat down. In a minute or so, still wearing her gloves, she went over to the counter and bought herself a cup of coffee.

She had not recognized the detectives as she walked past their table, nor had she seen me tablehopping and talking to many of the addicts. When I approached, her manner changed: She drew her shoulders back, tilted her head slightly, and gave me the bold come-on look of the seasoned hooker. When I explained about my article on addiction, she stared at me icily and then tuned out. Ignoring this, I sat down beside her and began to draw her out.

Underneath the icy exterior was a person who wanted to talk and relate. Her impregnable shell was a necessary armor and façade in the hard-knuckled world of junk. She had been used, beaten, and rejected too often to come off sounding like a shrinking violet. She said "lousy health" had kept her off the streets for the last couple of days. But she was able to scrounge some downers to keep her straight. Tonight she felt pretty good and hoped to pick up enough money for a shot.

Only three years had passed since she had graduated from a fine high school in New Jersey. Right after graduation she came to New York to her aunt's home. The idea of getting away from her parents thrilled her. She said her parents were too interested in making money. Their whole life was wrapped up in appearances, nothing real. They did things they didn't even like to do, just to make a good impression. She couldn't wait to get away. Her words were spilling out now, as if she was trying to get it all said before she was compelled to return to the silent tomb of addiction.

She realized she was not mature and had done many silly things in school. But she wasn't bad. She was only looking for the approval that should have been forthcoming from her parents. Her mischievous capers were just a way of projecting a little bit of herself in the hope of being noticed and accepted. She no longer had the courage or confidence to seek affection and friendship in a frank, open relationship; the risk of failure was too frightening. She had had her teachers all figured out too. She had known just how much each had to offer. Nicknames were even given to fit their varying degrees of incompetence. After she told me this, she seemed for a moment to become acutely aware of her own destitution, and as she looked at the floor, she said with a voice filled with irony, "Christ, look at me; I was miles ahead of them, wasn't I?"

Avoiding simple responsibilities as a teen-ager made her feel guilty—more because she disappointed her parents than herself. Still, being told her faults over and over again by her parents only drove her to look for ways to justify her disrespect, stubbornness, and disobedience. She started to doubt herself and wondered if her parents were right, and she hated them for it. They kept saying, "If you had only done what I had told you!" The thought that she didn't have anything worthwhile of herself to offer horrified her, and she fought back all the more to retain some independence and identity. The arguments became unbearable. She felt hemmed-in. She felt trapped. She felt so alone.

She met a young man in New York who was no substitute for her parents, but he gave the impression he was listening. She was vulnerable, deperately wanting to belong, to be liked, and he used this to his advantage. When drugs were offered, rather than refuse and risk being alone again, she went along. First marijuana and then harder drugs. Not long after, her boyfriend was sent to jail.

From that point, her loneliness was a deep pit from which she could never seem to escape. Joy was an element in her life long gone. This is one of the saddest aspects of an addict's life. Only a sharing with those we care about and love can make us joyful. An addict is not sure what he loves; often he cannot love. He has no joy.

The prophets of a chemical utopia evangelize the merits and benefits of drugs, which promise so much but give so little. One shot and you are riding on the crest of a wave, but when that wave recedes, the sludge and grime of yesterday's problems are still visible on the beach. Wholesome laughter is something that springs from the sudden incongruities of real life as presented to a rational mind. A brain abused and inundated by an inordinate use of drugs can only produce a sick hysteria or a delerious giggle. No joy, no honest-to-goodness happiness, no freedom. And this is the cruelest cut of all—to call these wretched slaves free agents doing their own thing. Edmund Burke made this point a long time ago when he said, "A person with an intemperate mind can never be free. His own passions forge his shackles."

The girl asked me for a cigarette and I didn't have any. One of the detectives noticed my predicament and flipped me a pack. When I offered her a cigarette, she took off one of the gloves she was wearing. Her hand was covered with abscesses and infections. I doubt if there were any veins left. She wore the pair of light, cloth gloves to hide her ugly hands. This is often a routine procedure when an attractive girl begins mainlining. Needle marks on her arms and shoulders would be like wearing a button announcing the fact that she was an addict. It would be very unattractive in the summer months when she wore skimpy dresses while hustling. Consequently, in an effort to stay visibly unmarked, she will shoot it up between the fingers, under the arms, in the buttocks, or in the lips of the vagina.

For many, the very thought of this is revolting. But now we are getting down to the nitty-gritty. This is exactly what addiction means. You can't picture yourself living in a flophouse and associating with down-and-out drug addicts, but if they were your means to the next shot, you would. It makes your skin crawl when you think of stabbing yourself with a needle, but if your body throbbed like an open sore and your brain was on fire, you would.

This girl had not only taken shots with a needle. When she didn't have works, a safety pin would do. She would just hit where she saw a scab or abscess and open it up.

Not too long ago she was going to football games as a member of the cheerleading squad. Not too long ago she was boy-crazy. Her whole pattern of life and dress was dictated by the latest male singing star or movie hero. Now her personality and interests had changed. She had to make seventy-five dollars a day to keep herself in dope. Now men were animals, and she felt they deserved to be treated as such. She took sadistic delight in shaming or embarrassing the men who paid for her sexual favors.

She lived in two little rooms, squalid and bare. When she had a customer, she would suddenly excuse herself for some reason and leave him for ten or fifteen minutes nervously waiting. Often she would light a cigarette at the most inopportune times, or giggle and belittle his groping advances. The physical reprisals from such antics often left her bruised and unable to work the streets.

Despite the dissolute life this girl was living, her background was incredibly conservative. The beatings she received from men were a self-imposed punishment for the growing guilt she felt about her addiction and actions. This pain cauterized her bleeding conscience and numbed the pangs of guilt temporarily.

I turned around and the two detectives were gone. The man at the table with us was asleep, and now the girl was on her feet. She asked me if I had any money. I gave her a dollar. Then she went through the pockets of the man who had come in with her, but only managed to siphon off a little change. "Cheap bastard," she muttered, and as if a word had never passed between us, she headed out the door to walk the streets. I started after her, but when I reached the sidewalk the detectives called to me and told me to let her go.

I watched her saunter down the dark street and thought of the family she still had in a nice little town in New Jersey. Suppose I had given a talk on narcotics to her class when she was a senior in high school and during the talk walked over to her and said, "In one year you'll be nothing but a junkie-prostitute hustling for nickels and dimes on the streets of New York." I'm sure the whole class would have roared with unbelieving laughter. How ridiculous! Something like that could never happen. Something like that could never . . .

11

Unexpected Arrivals

I rubbed a small spot clear on the greasy window and looked out at the row of dingy tenements across a Harlem street, each one projecting from the side of the other like a cancerous growth. The gutters were littered and the sidewalks marked with hopscotch squares and obscene chalking. My interest was drawn to four boys playing stoopball. The stoop the kids were playing on was empty, but all the rest had one or two older people hanging around. It was feeding time for the junkies and all these cats were waiting for the man with the big H.

Three Narcotics Squad detectives, one federal agent, and I were staked-out on the second floor of an old bus garage where we could clearly observe all the activity on the street below. Our prime target this evening was a pusher who had managed so far to elude the police twice. The neighborhood was being flooded with heroin, and the detectives were not sure of the pusher's identity.

By the way the addicts were gathering on the porches, we knew the pusher had to make his appearance soon, but there was no guarantee we would spot him. "He might be down there right now, Father. You'll know he's making his move when you see those junkies one by one start to split in different directions." All we could do was watch and wait, and on a stake-out that can sometimes run into days of surveillance.

The addicts across the way still shifted furtively. But there was no indication yet that anyone was making a score. The kids had stopped playing ball and had gone elsewhere. A menacing quiet seemed to prevail. Except for the addicts the street was strangely deserted, as if the people sensed the cat-and-mouse routine in operation. The junkies waited, and we waited.

The small, square windows of the garage started about five feet from the floor and went clear to the ceiling. The detectives had posted themselves down the line, each one squinting through the dirty panes. One of the detectives kept talking to me as his eyes scanned the buildings across the street. "If we have to make the bust out in the open, Father, you stay close to the side of the building; that's the safest place. Sometimes the people throw things out the windows at us when they see us making an arrest. Besides, we wouldn't want anything to happen to that porkpie hat." He grinned, and slapped me on the back. This particular detective always smoked a pipe. He looked more like an Oxford professor than a narcotics detective.

Suddenly a few minutes later he silently pointed to one of the addicts sitting on the stoop directly across from us. He had gotten up slowly, walked over to a garbage can, taken a brown paper bag from the can, then gone back and sat down on some newspapers he had spread on the step. In a quick motion we almost missed, he flipped the bag over his shoulder into the hallway behind him. "That must be junk in the bag, Father, but I don't think he's the pusher we want. Evidently, the boy we want already made his drop." The young boy got up again and folded the newspapers he had been sitting on and tucked them under his arm. He began to saunter indifferently down the street stopping for a few seconds at this group and then another. The entire street came alive. Addicts started to "shake" the scene in every direction. "He's telling them where their bag of junk is, Father." I watched them scurry off and wondered how many times they had gone through the same agonizing routine. There were about twenty addicts in all. That means there were really about forty. Whenever I see a group of junkies I always double the number, because before a junkie dies he or she always entices at least one more into the world of living death.

A white sedan with New Jersey license plates burst onto the scene and came screeching to a halt right below us—the front part of the car dipped down to the street and then snapped back in a rocking motion. A man jumped out of the back seat and ran into the first floor of the bus garage. Later we surmised that he had gone to the toilet, and then slipped away when he saw us coming down the ramp. We were immediately suspicious of this car because all three of the men in the car were white, and our stake-out was taking place in a solidly black neighborhood. The men in the front seat didn't move. Then from the hallway across the street a young man appeared. He was carrying a brown paper bag similar to the one that was tossed into the same hallway about fifteen minutes before. I could feel the tension start to build. The detectives were quickly setting up their strategy. "Father, we may have to move out of her fast, so be ready to go." I watched the young man with the brown paper bag walk down the steps of the porch and head directly for the white car on our side of the street. When he reached the car he dropped the bag in the lap of the driver, turned on his heel, and took off down the street in the opposite direction.

"That's it, Father, let's go!" We all started to run down

the circular ramp to the ground floor. Two detectives darted out the side door of the garage where the car was parked. I followed the other detective and the agent out the front door. This flanking operation placed the car between the two groups. When we hit the sidewalk, we saw that the white sedan had already pulled up to the corner, so we headed straight for it. The driver saw us coming and jammed his foot down on the accelerator. Too late he remembered the car was still in reverse. The car shot backward, crashing into an oncoming bus. This briefly interrupted the driver's getaway attempt. Before we could reach the car he had put it in drive and was careening through the intersection while feverishly cramming the small glassine bags down his throat in an effort to swallow them. We started running after the car. One of the detectives fired two warning shots into the air while shouting for them to stop. With one rear tire flat from the collision with the bus the car swerved out of control until it finally bounced off a telephone pole and came to an abrupt stop.

In seconds the detectives had the two men out and were frisking them. The "two men" turned out to be very young boys of seventeen and eighteen.

The detectives were searching all over the street and in the car for the bags of narcotics. "Every junkie in the neighborhood will be out here after we leave, Father, looking for any bags we might have overlooked." We found about twelve bags, but the detectives were certain there must have been more. They ripped out the lining of the car and looked under the seats and behind the hubcaps. Then I heard one of the detectives say, "Hey, look at this." There in the crease between the fender and the hood were eleven bags of heroin. They had spilled onto the fender and spaced themselves almost perfectly. The white powder against the white car made them barely visible.

My interest was focused on the two boys. One of them

was shaking like a leaf and crying. The other boy, the driver, showed no emotion. Both of them had their hands on the roof of the car and I noticed what looked like track marks on their arms. The detectives handcuffed them and were about to put them into the police car when the more stoic of the two got sick all over the sidewalk—and the detectives added six more bags of heroin to the collection. Junkies will try anything to save or hide their precious dope. Some of the more exotic methods are swallowing it, inserting it into the rectum or vagina, or wearing it in menstrual napkins or tampons. Any sensibilities a person might have possessed before drug abuse are ancient history once they become hooked.

When we arrived at the police station, I stayed in the background while the detectives went through the standard routine. Both boys were seniors at the same high school in New Jersey. The driver, Gus, was very bitter. As young as he was, it sounded as if life had tied his guts in knots. He answered every question with an obscene remark or gesture. Meanwhile, his buddy, Alby, was docile and meekly answered all questions.

They both had a sallow, unhealthy look, but they did not appear to be real strung-out junkies yet. After absorbing a few profanities from Gus, while trying to engage in a conversation, I called Alby aside. He was really shaken by the whole thing. In an effort to gain his confidence, I told him I was a priest. His eyes got as wide as saucers, and I thought his lower jaw would touch the floor. Excitedly, he turned and yelled to the other boy, "Hey, Gus, he's a priest!" It was the first remark that had stopped Gus cold—he stared at me and I looked back at him unflinchingly until he turned away. But the next second he was bending over me asking, "Father, you have to help us, our parents don't know anything about this." The curtain was down on the hard-nosed act; now it was con-artist time. Even if I had

had the power to let that boy walk out the front door that moment, he probably would have gone looking for a bag of junk. As much as I knew he would try to use me any way he could, I felt sorry for him. And if what he said about his parents not knowing were true, I felt sorry for them also. Alby's spirits were somewhat elevated once he knew I was a priest. Now he had someone to talk to who would listen. He told me of his introduction to drugs. It began in the hospital after he had undergone a very serious operation. The pain was terrible, so they used to give him shots of morphine and, later on, pills. When he left the hospital, he continued to take pills and finally started using heroin. He had only been taking heroin for the past two months. Then Gus spoke up reluctantly, but with a tinge of inner pride, and told me he started just for kicks one summer, sniffing glue at the beach under the boardwalk. This is how they got their "joy." "One time I really sniffed a 'sockful' and had a total 'flake-out,' man [became mentally disorientated]. When I got straight, my buddies told me I almost beat up my girlfriend; they had to hold me down. That scared me, so I didn't sniff for a while."

He played this game for almost the whole summer until one day his nose swelled up and his head throbbed. He told his parents he had banged his nose playing basketball. His head hurt so badly he could hardly see, so he started taking some downers. At a drive-in movie one night a "friend" took a set of works from under the seat and asked him if he wanted to try. He'd been galloping horse ever since.

Two years ago if I had asked either of these teen-agers where they would be this day, they would have mentioned all sorts of wonderful places. Instead they were in a police station in a sleazy part of New York, answering to the inglorious title of junkie. Two years ago, the world was theirs; now their future was in jeopardy. So young and the remainder of their life in such a state of doubt.

I asked Gus, "Do you want to kick it?"

"What for?"

"For one thing, it's gotten you into a lot of trouble."

"This is the first time."

"When is the last time you went to church?"

"About six months ago maybe."

"Are you losing your faith in God too?"

"Does God believe in me?"

"Seems I've heard that before somewhere. What exactly do you want God to do for you?"

"I think people who go to church are a bunch of phonies, a bunch of secret creeps."

"How do you see yourself?"

"At least I'm not hurting nobody but me."

That same concept is phrased differently over and over again. People say, "It's my body, I can do whatever I want with it."

It's your body all right, on this we agree. Now as to what you can do with that body, here we need some clarification. For instance, you can do whatever you want with your feet, as long as they don't walk on my property. You can do whatever you want with your hands, as long as they don't steal my coat. You can do whatever you want with your eyes, as long as they don't invade my privacy. You can do whatever you want with your tongue, as long as you tell the truth. In other words, as someone once said, you are absolutely and totally free to do whatever you want up until the point where you can touch your neighbor's nose.

Somebody once asked Daniel Webster for the single most important thought of his lifetime. He answered, "The most important thought I ever had was my individual responsibility to God." We must always remember that we are dependent beings; dependent first on God, and then on each other. This dependency gives us responsibilities, and in proportion these curtail our personal freedoms. We have a responsibility to safeguard the lives of others when we drive; therefore, we are not free to take drugs that will make us unsafe drivers. We have a responsibility to help maintain law and order in the community; therefore, we are not free to take drugs that will lead us to disrupt the community. We have a responsibility as members of the human race to contribute to the human society; therefore, we are not free to use drugs that will frustrate, distort, or destroy that capability. Anytime we do anything that infringes on the rights and freedoms of others, we are not acting according to our personal rights and freedoms, but, rather, with unbridled license or cruel aggression.

Our bodies were given to us for two reasons: first, to give honor and glory to God as the Creator, and second, to act as a finely tuned instrument through which the beautiful sounds of our soul can be played. Any deed that affects these two ends in a deleterious manner is irresponsible and should not be committed. So really, the statement "It's my body, I can do whatever I want with it" wouldn't even be true for the last person on earth. Therefore, the personal misuse of drugs is an unrestrained and selfish independence that can only culminate in the obliteration of the peace and happiness that we have a right and a freedom to pursue.

One of the detectives brought over the telephone numbers of the boys' parents and asked if I wanted to call them. Gus and Alby looked at each other, realizing that the moment of truth was a phone call away. Their fears were well-founded. Their parents reacted with a combination of shock, outrage, fear, and dispair—and of course the inevitable questions: "Why my child?—What happens now?" The detectives told me to discourage them from coming over to Harlem—they'd see their sons in court the next morning.

We took Gus and Alby down to the precinct lockup. At

best precinct lockups are cruddy and stinking. When Gus and Alby heard the somber and lonesome sounds of clanging iron doors they looked petrified. Taking advantage of the situation, I said, "Go ahead, look around, this is your home. You might as well get used to it. They're going to be opening and closing that steel door behind you until one day they get tired and throw the key away. This is the home that junk made, and you're the only one that can change it." They moved inside with the detective; and the door clanged behind them. I had the feeling they would never be back to this place or any place like it.

I prayed, and I knew they were praying harder.

12

Just a Boy

The newer police stations in the boroughs of Greater New York, built of steel, glass, and cement, can be severe, impersonal places—their history is yet to be recorded. The older precinct houses, survivors from the early days of the century, from the Prohibition era, from the Depression days, have grown old with the troubles and grief of generations. Their battered, peeling walls are haunted by a brand of cynicism and melancholy peculiarly their own.

I remember sitting in just such an old precinct house one night, dressed in faded denims, baggy sweatshirt, and docker's boots. Tilted back in a swivel chair, feet propped-up on a rusty rolltop desk, I looked more like an off-duty stevedore than a priest. I was idling away the time, waiting for two narcotics detectives to finish their paperwork before the evening patrol, when a uniformed policeman brought a thin, wiry, gray-haired woman into the room. She asked to speak with a Narcotics Squad detective. One of the plain-clothes men I was waiting for introduced himself and asked her to sit down. She moved quietly into a chair and began talking.

She told us how the day before she had met her neighbor and friend in the supermarket. Her friend was upset because her sixteen-year-old son was using drugs. She had suspected it a few months ago, but he denied it. She said this mother went on to say she had done everything she knew to persuade the boy to stop. Now the boy was stealing to get money for the drugs. He had already dropped out of school. The mother didn't know where to turn. But she said if the boy came home that night, she was going to lock him in his room so he couldn't get out. With genuine concern showing in her gentle features, the woman said she had not seen the boy at all that day and usually she saw him once or twice. This made her worry. Maybe the mother had done something foolish. Finally, she decided to come and ask the police what they thought.

The detectives assured her she had done the right thing. The woman asked that her name not be mentioned. Under the circumstances, this was understandable. We took the name and address of the mother and the detectives said they would do what they could to help. One of the detectives walked the woman to the door and mentioned that they would call her if they needed any further information.

When the woman had gone, the detectives quickly cleared the desk of the reports they had been working on. Most likely just a routine case, but both of them agreed it wouldn't do any harm to take a ride and investigate.

On the way out the front door I was introduced to another member of the Narcotics Squad. She was a stately and strikingly beautiful girl. I was told that she was presently working undercover on a very important case. She figured prominently in an operation that could bust someone very high up in the illegal narcotics echelon. She looked just like any other girl, but obviously, or rather not so obviously, she was a highly trained policewoman, doing an extremely dangerous job. You just never think there are people like that around, except in the cloak-and-dagger movies. I asked her if her job frightened her. She laughed and said, "All the time!" She was a very brave girl. I told her I would keep her in my prayers. She smiled and said, "Thank you," and then hurried inside.

As we drove over to check out the woman's suspicion, the detectives were discussing the possibilities of the situation. They had heard of similar cases where the family precipitated a showdown and the addict was forced to do something desperate, like taking a hurried fix and winding up with a fatal overdose. Hundreds of kids below the age of eighteen die every year of overdoses from drugs. I wonder how many families whose children are not involved in drug abuse ever think of that. Over six hundred people died from overdoses last year just in New York alone.

In a few minutes we were smack in the middle of one of the neighborhoods claimed by the famous Dead End Kids. But the trouble we would find might not be the harmless roughneck kind we saw in those old movies. The place where the woman lived was shabby and rundown. There were high tenements with narrow canyonlike alleys, just wide enough to make an interesting jump for kids who didn't have much to do but climb roofs on a Saturday afternoon.

After you are in New York for a while, you begin to realize that a separate world exists on those rooftops. I already knew this. When I was a kid we'd say "Let's go climbing." And we would climb everything in sight. We would jump from roof to roof, sometimes going the length of a whole block. It was a crazy thing to do, but I can still remember the thrill I felt as I sailed across those open alleyways. In New York, maybe more than any other place, roofs become a refuge, a meeting place, a tar-bubbled beach, an imaginary bluff where a person can view a make-believe kingdom. Only a roof four stories from the ground, but it can make that crowded, noisy world seem a thousand miles away. No spot in the city can claim more neutrality or offer greater sanctuary to the tired urban spirit. And yet, unfortunately, this peaceful, secluded oasis has been the scene where more than one young addict has gotten his first taste of drugs.

We pressed the buzzer to the apartment, and the door was opened by a little girl six or seven years old. The mother came right on the heels of the girl. The detectives identified themselves and asked if they could come in and talk to her. The woman motioned us in. She seemed very nervous and upset. A radio was blaring loudly, and the kids who were in another room came out and stood around staring. There were seven children. Quite a brood for what looked like tight living quarters. They were poor, but everything was clean and so were the children. For some reason the atmosphere seemed foreboding. I didn't know exactly why, but I had the distant feeling something was very wrong. The detectives asked the woman if her son was home. She said no and explained that he was staying at her sister's house. When the detectives inquired if she knew that her son was taking drugs, she started to cry and emphatically denied having any knowledge of the boy's using drugs.

She was a short, stocky woman with dark hair. Her hands had a leathery sheen that betrayed a lifetime of hard work. Her bearing was rooted, and her pinched mouth presented an intimidating expression. A cursory judgment, indeed, but I had no doubt as to who was boss in that family. She was sobbing uncontrollably now and began berating us for not being out trying to catch real criminals, instead of persecuting a small boy. All of a sudden she lunged toward one of the smaller children. But it was too late. Before the mother reached him, the boy had flipped a latch and opened the door to what looked like a pantry. She had stumbled and fallen to one knee. As I reached to help her up she kept repeating over and over, "I didn't know what to do." One of the detectives went over and pushed the door wide open.

A naked teen-age boy lay face down on the floor in a pool of his own greenish vomit. Beads of sweat and blood glistened on his thin body in the dim light of the single bulb dangling from the ceiling. His left ankle, shackled to the leg of the iron bed, was suspended in mid-air, and the short chain twisted around his leg was bloody where it had torn the flesh as he fell. On the foot of the bed above the chain hung a rosary. A plastic crucifix glowed faintly on the wall over the head of the bed. One of the detectives knelt beside him to take his pulse while his partner checked his ankle for a possible fracture. The boy was barely conscious, his breathing shallow and labored, his frail body wracked periodically with violent tremors and spasms of dry heaving. He was kicking heroin "cold turkey."

I picked him up and it was like carrying a bundle of sticks thinly wrapped. He was so frail, so delicate. I told the mother to get me some blankets, and one of the detectives asked her for the key to the lock on the chain. The boy was soaking wet with sweat and blood. He had broken a glass that was on a small table and cut his arms with it. In severe withdrawal, sometimes even the sensation of something sharp cutting into the skin is symbolic of the needle, and this brings some sort of relief.

I quickly sponged him off and wrapped him in the warm blankets on the bed. His body was calmer now . . . the chills and spasms were lessening. Without anyone noticing, I gave him Conditional Absolution. It was difficult to believe that this frail, undersized boy was sixteen. When I made the Sign of the Cross over him, he opened his eyes. Frightened and bewildered at seeing two strange men staring at him, he whispered his mother's name and asked for a little water.

The track marks on his body made it evident that he was mainlining heroin.

What the mother had done was to try to cold turkey her son. She didn't know the term, but she had heard that if you keep addicts away from drugs for a while, they lose their craving. It meant she was going to force her son to go through narcotic withdrawal symptoms until the boy's body no longer needed drugs physically. This method of detoxification does not involve a gradual withdrawal; rather, it is a sharp and brutal halt to all narcotics entering the system.

The process can be a risky business. The body can respond to this sudden privation in a very violent manner. Members of The American Medical Association, in an article entitled "Opium Addiction," have recorded a graphic account of what cold turkey can mean. They relate: "As the time approaches for what would have been the addict's next administration of the drug, one notices that he glances frequently in the direction of the clock and manifests a certain degree of restlessness. If the administration is omitted, he begins to move about in a rather aimless way, failing to remain in one position long. He is either in bed, sitting on a chair, standing up, or walking about, constantly changing from one to another. With this restlessness, yawning soon appears, which becomes more and more violent. At the end of a period of about eight hours, restlessness becomes marked. He will throw himself onto a bed, curl up, and wrap the blankets tightly around his shoulders, sometimes burying his head in the pillows. For a few minutes, he will toss from side to side and then suddenly jump out of the bed and start to walk back and forth, head bowed, shoulders stooping. This lasts only a few minutes. He may then lie on the floor close to the radiator, trying to keep warm. Even here he is not contented, and he either resumes his pacing about or again throws himself onto the bed, wrapping himself under heavy blankets. At the same time he complains bitterly of suffering with cold and then hot flashes, but mostly chills. He breathes like a person who is cold, in short jerky powerful respirations. His skin shows the characteristic pilimotor activity well-known to those persons as cold turkey. The similarity of the skin at this stage to that of a plucked turkey is striking. Coincident of this feeling of chilliness, he complains of being unable to breathe through his nose. Nasal secretion is excessive. He has a most abject appearance, but is fairly docile in his behavior. This is a picture of his appearance during the first eight hours.

"Subsequently, lachrymation, yawning, sneezing, and chilliness are extreme. A feeling of suffocation at the back of the throat is frequently mentioned. Usually at this stage, the addict complains of cramps, locating them most frequently in the abdomen, but often in the back and lower extremities. . . . Vomiting and diarrhea appear. He may vomit large quantities of bile-stained fluid. Perspiration is excessive. Muscular twitchings are commonly present; they may occur anywhere, but are most violent in the lower extremities."

The shock can bring on severe twitching, convulsions, heavy sweating, chills, cramps, bleeding from the nose, ears, and mouth, and empty vomiting. Such aggravated symptoms, as described above, have even caused deep coma and death.

However, withdrawal can also be no worse than having a bad cold or flu. The severity depends on how long the person has been mainlining, the purity of the heroin, the addict's age, the general strength of an addict's constitution, and, perhaps, having in his possession a couple of barbiturates to lessen the pain. Most heroin today is cut so badly, the junkies call it garbage. If nothing but garbage has been injected, then the addict may have an easier time in cold turkey. Taking all this into consideration, the mother took a terrible chance without realizing the odds.

She really could not be blamed. What she did was done in desperation—an emotional act, rather than a willful one. Quite possibly, it might even have been an unconscious expression of her complete dominance over the boy—a dominance that may well have destroyed his psychological well-being, long before dope had crushed him physically. Such a poor relationship could easily have triggered in her mind a self-righteous extreme meant to rectify the worst on a long list of failures credited to the boy. No one who has ever counseled an addict fails to perceive how often the underlying causes of addiction are spawned by psychological scars received in childhood.

John Ruskin once uttered some penetrating words in this regard. He said: "The human soul in youth is not a machine of which you can polish the cogs with any kelp or brickdust near at hand. The whole period of youth is one essentially of formation, edification, instruction; intaking of stores, establishment of vital habits, hopes and faiths. There is not an hour of it but is trembling with destiny."

Other parents react differently from this mother in similar drug situations. They refuse to believe. They place a canopy of unreality over the whole crisis. Just a bad dream from which they are going to awaken any minute. An attitude indigenous, perhaps, to not having taken their children seriously enough in the past. However, this is one time the adolescent may be grateful for not being taken seriously. It allows him to continue to use drugs.

She was cleaning the boy and kissing and hugging him at the same time. A man came into the apartment and identified himself as the boy's father. He said there was no need for an ambulance. He had called the doctor, and they would take care of the boy. The detectives were relieved that there were no narcotics in the house that would make the boy liable to arrest. They explained that he would not have to go to jail for being an addict. Under federal law a person can only be arrested for illegal possession and sale of narcotics. However, the parents would have to come to the precinct house in the morning and give a full report.

As we stood there watching the mother and boy, I could not help but notice the expressions on the faces of the detectives. How often they are reputed to be hard cops. At this point the description could not have been more inept. They were as moved as I was by this tragic episode.

The thought that disturbed and agitated me most was who had sold this kid a bill of goods? "Come on, man, try it! Don't you have no soul, no heart?" How many times had he heard those goading words?

Here was a boy who should have been worried about whether or not he was going to make the basketball team, or get a date with that pretty little girl who sat two seats ahead of him in school. He should have been worried about pimples, a part in the school play, or how he was going to get his pesty sister off his back. Instead, he was worried about where he was going to get enough "bread" for the next cooker full of garbage.

Two sets of worries: One set would have placed him in that delightful world filled with the painful luxuries of being an adolescent; a time of adjustment and scary insecurity. Those wonderful, turbulent years when small things break your heart, and big things bore you stiff.

Later on I was to learn from the man who ran the paperstand on the corner that the boy had not only turned to thievery, but had also become a male prostitute. Older men seeking sexual favors from a young boy were a good source of income to sustain his habit.

He was on a rotten treadmill where being sixteen years old did not matter. He was, quite probably, living out the last few years of his life with no time for living. He was too occupied just trying to stay alive in a world where living means barest survival. He was alone. He was old. He was spent. He was just a boy.

13

A Better Life

When an eighteen-year-old addict tells me she is coughing up blood, that she can't touch her sides because the pain is so severe, and that her hair is falling out, I begin to wish she were talking not just to me but to every politician in the country; getting under their skins and taunting them to honestly consider the drug problem. I begin to wish she could be booked into every rock festival in the country to belt out the awful truth that drug abuse is anything but fun and games. I begin to wish she could sit in every home across the nation, so parents could see and hear first-hand what will become of their children unless they get together and put a stop to the nonsense of letting kids rule the country.

But as it was, I was the only one listening to this girl. And we were not in a politician's office or at a rock festival or in someone's living room. We were standing in the doorway of a tenement in Brooklyn.

She had called me earlier that day, and because she sounded so desperate I had driven out to see her that very night. Her family's apartment was very small, so to have some privacy we spoke in the doorway of the building.

She told me she used to watch her older brother shoot it up, and one day decided to try it herself. Just for kicks. She got more of a kick than she expected, and she liked it. That was a year and a half ago. She had struggled along so far on the money her mother gave her, and once in a while she would go into the lobby of a big hotel and "boost" (steal) luggage.

She had been doing this with much success for over six months now. But her appetite for drugs was growing, and the money she obtained from fencing the different stolen articles was not enough. Her only recourse was prostitution and the very idea revolted her. She was ready to do anything to kick the habit rather than become a streetwalker.

Her older brother never came home anymore. He spent his time in and out of jail. When she said this about her brother, it brought to mind what an ex-addict had once told me. He said he had wanted very much to help his younger cousin, who was heading for the drug scene, "But every time he needed me, I was in jail. Now he's on junk and I regret that very much."

He lived on the streets, she went on to say, and she was sure he would eventually shoot up a bad dose. Without meaning to, she started to sound like a solicitous big sister. For a while I lost sight of the fact that it was her problem I had come to discuss.

We continued talking, and as I stood there in that darkened doorway it struck me that we were actually discussing this girl's mortal destiny. What she was doing could only lead to self-destruction. A determined step had to be taken in the opposite direction. It was a pity that such a life-and-death crisis had to be faced by an eighteen year old. The thought occurred to me that maybe I would like to see her speak before some of our Christian educators. Perhaps she might succeed in ramming home the simple truth that for every act you perform, you must be ready to absorb the consequences, good or bad. When I hear some of the pap that is taught to younger children, I wonder how they grow up with any sense of responsibility at all.

Kids grow up with the impression that they can do anything as long as their motive is love and their action is positive. Transfer that undisciplined philosophy to the use of drugs and you have a difficult time trying to convince young people that the abuse of drugs is not good. It becomes impossible when they tell you they are doing it to increase their capacity to love and thereby make a positive contribution to society. I have seen some such lovers and I have noted their contributions as they lay dead from an overdose in a squalid alley.

I asked the girl if she would be able to see me the next day. I told her I would see if I could make some arrangements to get her into a hospital. My hands were brittle from the cold as I scratched the appointment time down on a piece of paper I had in my pocket. I told her to pray very hard, that we needed all the help we could get. She nodded, said "Thanks," and went upstairs.

I flipped my coat collar up tightly around my neck and braced myself against the brisk wind. As I started walking toward the car I heard, "Hey, can you help us?" I turned and saw two young men walking toward me. The bigger of the two said, "What ya doing?" I didn't answer him, but kept heading for the car. I was glad the girl had gone upstairs. I didn't know exactly what was going to happen, but I couldn't think of anything good. If I could just make the car, I'd jump in, lock the door, and "burn rubber." The car was just a few yards away now. I was praying someone else would show up on this deserted street.

I decided to make a dash for the car, but I hadn't gone two steps when I felt one of them grab me from behind. I swung around and pushed him against the car. The thud forced a good whiff of alcohol into my face. I broke loose and turned around just in time to feel the other one's fist crash into my forehead. This sent me sprawling. I quickly got to my feet, and between dragging and pulling did the best I could to work my way to the car door. We bounced and scrapped a couple of more times until somehow I lunged toward the car and broke free. I opened the door, slammed and locked it. The sound of that motor was music to my ears. As I slammed it into drive I noticed out of the corner of my eye that one of them had a gun. I crouched down in the seat, stepped on the gas, and prayed. The back wheels spun and the car lurched ahead. As I raced out to the main street, I heard two shots. I slouched lower and made a howling, screeching turn onto the main drag. I don't know how fast I was traveling. I didn't care. The sight of people at the first intersection gave me a wonderful sensation of being safe again.

I couldn't believe it had happened. I took a couple of deep breaths to settle myself down. Every part of me was still shaking. I wondered if I was hurt. I looked in the rear-view mirror. No scratches or cuts, just a knot on my forehead. Suddenly, I felt very sick. I pulled over to the side and opened the door. Blood was on my hand and dirt all over my clothes. I started brushing off my overcoat and noticed that I still had it buttoned tightly around the neck with the collar pulled up. As drunk as those two guys were, I was sure they didn't know I was a priest. The overcoat hid my Roman collar.

The next day the young girl came to my office. I mentioned nothing about the incident the night before. I told her that I had been trying to get her admitted to a hospital. At that time most hospitals would not even accept addicts, and those that did had a waiting list a mile long.

The task of supplying aid to a person dependent on drugs can be a frustrating one. And in this case the frustration was increased by the addict herself. As I looked at the girl she seemed different from the night before. She was distant and uneasy.

"Father, I don't think I can kick it; I don't know if I want to," she said.

"What made you change your mind?"

"I don't know. I don't like the things I do, but I like the dope. I like the way it feels. I don't know if I can kick it, Father."

You could almost have visualized this poor kid being squeezed in a giant vise. She mentioned something about a job. She was really grasping at straws. She would never be able to hold down a job. The thought of trying to make it without drugs terrified her. This is one more indication of the stranglehold of addiction.

There are many junkies on the street right now who do not want help. Many are willing to spend a year in jail rather than give up their habit. How many young people at this moment who have never tried dope can conceive of themselves in jail? The very thought of it is ridiculous. But this is exactly what can happen once addiction takes hold.

I kept her talking. She seemed to relax more when she spoke, even though she still had a nervous catch in her voice. A sadness came over her whenever I mentioned religion. She had deep feelings of guilt in this area. She was concerned that God would never forgive her, that she would lose her soul. Sometimes when she thought she was dying, she would panic and shout out loud all kinds of prayers. Once after using a dirty and clogged set of works she was so sick that she promised God she would never take dope again if He would make her well. Two days later, she was shooting up. This made her guilt more oppressive and gave her greater reason to punish herself with drugs.

We had a small chapel right across the hall from my office, and I asked her if she would visit with me. I said,

"Maybe the Good Lord will help us both come up with some answers." She entered the chapel like a guest who feels unwelcome. We both made our reverence to the Blessed Sacrament and knelt in the back pew, each praying our own prayers. Then we sat back and continued to talk. She said she once spent three weeks in a hospital getting detoxified. The day she left she bought four bags of heroin from a nurse's aide.

When she mentioned the nurse's aide, I knew exactly what the girl was talking about. This girl was a junkie, yes, but she was not yet demoralized. But some existing rehabilitation facilities and detention centers are real snakepits. Send a girl like this in and she comes out ten times worse. Overcrowding, coed toilets, poor discipline, dope smuggling, prostitution, the whole sordid scene takes place right behind the front door. And yet, when politicians are stumping the luncheon circuit, these very facilities are mentioned in the same breath with the word "rehabilitation." Making it look good on paper is the oldest dodge in the world.

She went on to say that things weren't much better at the high school she attended. She was sure the teachers knew the kids were taking drugs but just did nothing about it. The school had a place underneath the stage where chairs were stored for assemblies. Girls would sell themselves there for a dollar or fifty cents and then use the money for junk. She said it wasn't hard to buy dope around the school once they got to know you. "In the beginning, just to keep you honest and make sure you're not the Man, the pusher will sell you a beat bag or dummy. This don't have no dope in it, just some kind of white powder. If you're tastin', you come back hollerin' for a good bag, and then he knows you're cool." If an undercover man makes a buy like that, often his cover is burned because of the time it takes the police laboratory to analyze it as a beat bag. The pusher figures a real addict would have been back much sooner.

This girl had been the whole drug route with the exception of prostitution. Now she was considering that step.

I was about to ask her about this when she said, "Father, can I go to Confession?" This threw me a little off balance. She seemed so despairing about the mercy of God, I never expected her to ask for Confession. I walked over to the Confessional, opened the door, and stepped inside. As I sat there in the quiet darkness I asked God to give her the courage to say what she so much wanted to say, and to give me the wisdom to help her. This would be a difficult Confession to make, since she had probably not done so for a long time. It would not be a question of asking her to do penance for her sins. She had already lashed her conscience into a state of despair. If I could only convince her that God really cares, really loves, really forgives, she might begin feeling like a decent person, a worthwhile human being, someone who has something to offer without the help of drugs. After a few minutes, I stood up and opened the door of the Confessional. The chapel was empty. She was gone.

The next afternoon I drove over to where she lived, but no one was home. I even sat in the car for half an hour thinking she might show up, but she never came. For two weeks I made every effort to get in touch with her, without luck. Once I found her mother at home and she told me her daughter hardly ever slept at home any more. It was more convenient for her to go to work every day if she stayed at a friend's house. She had gotten a job and was doing very well—her mother showed me a television set the daughter had given her a few days previously. I left my name and telephone number with her and asked her to give them to her daughter the next time she came home. I said I was very happy to hear things were going so nicely and I left.

I knew in my own heart what was going on and so did the mother. We were just playing games with each other. A month went by without my hearing from the girl. Then one night I was sitting in on a wiretap with three detectives when I got a call from the precinct house. An addict who had been picked up said that he knew me and wanted to see me.

He was standing in the small lockup cage in the corner of the room. I walked over and said, "I'm Father Melody; did you want to see me?" He looked at me blankly for a few seconds, and then as if he had suddenly popped back into reality said, "Yes, you know my sister. I tried to tell her, Father. You gotta do somethin'. She's hustlin', Father. No good, no good."

This was the addict-brother the girl had told me about the night we talked in front of her house. It was difficult getting information from him since he was half-stoned. He said she kept moving from place to place, so he didn't know where she lived, but he gave me the names of the streets she usually worked. According to him she was sick and needed help.

Two nights later I was sitting with two detectives across the street from a dingy hotel watching the steady stream of junkie-prostitutes file in and out with their customers in hot pursuit. I felt very sorry for those girls. Sure, most are hard and cold. But narcotics has driven many of them to do something they detest. They hate themselves and they hate the world that sneers at them. How awful it must be to stand there and know that most of the people passing by consider you the scum of society. An addict once told me she almost went out of her mind when she was forced to resort to prostitution.

So much misery. How lonely they must feel. How hollow and empty as they stand there waiting to be used and abused by people who couldn't care whether they lived or died. What yearnings must well up inside a young addict-prostitute when she sees students pass by, carefree and gay, with possible horizons and goals that capture the imagination. Narcotics, for the time being, has carved out her horizon—a six-by-fifteen room with a smelly old man who drools on her shoulders.

I looked at my watch. We had been waiting for an hour and a half. One of the detectives suggested we drive through the neighborhood. "Sometimes a hustler won't use a hotel, Father. They might go in cars or use the exit stairways of big hotels. Maybe we can spot her on the street." We cruised for about twenty minutes without any luck and decided to call it a night. I gave the detective her description and asked them to do what they could to find her. I was positive they would do a much more thorough job of looking if I were not along.

Two nights later they took me to a small coffeeshop not far from Times Square. One of the detectives stayed in the car and the other walked over to the window of the shop with me. "Is that her, Father?"

She was sitting in a booth with two other hustlers. A blonde wig changed her appearance, but it was her all right. When I walked into the shop, her face went white in recognition. She got up immediately and walked outside. I followed her. The detective advised me, "Father, if you're going to talk to her, you better take her into the car. You never know who might see you and get the wrong idea." At that the girl interrupted, "I'm not going in any car. You can't bust me. I haven't done anything. Leave me alone. Father, I'm not ready." I said, "You're sick, you're going to kill yourself." "I'm not sick. I'm okay, just leave me alone." I stood there talking to her for about fifteen minutes, but nothing I could say made any difference. She didn't want my help. At least, she said she didn't. Finally, she promised to call me in a couple of days. The call never came and I never saw or heard from her again. The detectives said that she must have gone to another city. I always prayed that she had gone to a better life, a life away from drugs.

14

No Exceptions

As a nurse she had given thousands of injections. Now, once again she was plying her skill. Placing the arm on a clean towel, she tied off the circulation just below the biceps with a rubber tourniquet and impatiently watched for a vein to bulge in the bend of the elbow. Then she sponged the throbbing vein with a cool alcohol-soaked pad. The needle slipped in smoothly and professionally, making the arm sparkle with a pleasurable tingling sensation. This time it was her arm, and it was smooth and white. She watched her delicate skin hug the needle tightly and felt her vein suck in the deadening drug as she flushed the syringe empty. Ripping off the tourniquet, the sudden dramatic release from tension was like bursting a bag of puss pressing down on the brain. She slumped in her chair.

Two years ago if someone had told her that she would get an erotic feeling from must having the point of a needle puncture her skin, she would have laughed. Now, the very act of holding a syringe filled with morphine produced rapturous anticipation. Not too long ago she was interested only in the betterment of humanity and increasing her love of God, for she was a nurse and a Catholic nun. But now she was also a drug addict.

I had received a call from Sister Julia several months after lecturing informally on narcotics addiction to a group of her sister nuns at St. Joseph's Shrine. We arranged to meet at the information desk of the hospital where she lived and worked. When I arrived, I had her paged. Almost immediately a small nun in her early thirties wearing the traditional habit of her Community approached me and introduced herself. I noticed, as we walked toward a small office near the nurses' station, that her eyes were almost obscured by the large, thick, tinted lenses of her glasses.

As we settled into chairs, she folded her hands on the small desk in front of her and spoke thoughtfully: "I've done a great deal of serious thinking this past week, Father, and I don't know how else to put it, other than to say, I'm a drug addict." I was thunderstruck.

"What do you mean, you're an addict?"

"Just that, Father. I take injections of morphine every few hours throughout the day. It's getting worse. I'm afraid sooner or later I'll be caught and the scandal to the Community, the hospital, and my family will be terrible!"

Though it was only midmorning, I could see that she was already getting jumpy and would soon need another shot.

"Where do you go to take your shots?"

"It depends, Father. We live upstairs on the top floor of the hospital. During the day when it's crowded around the nurses' station, I go up to my room. But on the night shift, when things are quiet, I take it right in the narcotics closet where we keep the drug cabinet."

The whole business seemed so unlikely. I can understand angry people who take drugs out of protest and get trapped; people with mystical delusions who get psyched into the drug scene; young people who are bored; kids without parents; but a nun! The realization struck home that there are no sacred cows, no untouchables. Anyone, no matter what vocation or rank, can be crushed under the merciless heel of drug abuse. You may win for a while, but you are eventually doomed to a living death. Taking drugs is a cat-and-mouse game, and it becomes very obvious who plays the role of the mouse.

The tears began to flow down her cheeks, and she took off her glasses to wipe her eyes with a handkerchief.

"It all began two years ago when I was finishing my work for my nursing degree at summer school. . . . The pressures were unbearable. I was carrying too many credits . . . had too many term papers to write . . . oral exams were a week away . . . there was never time for study, much less sleep. Then, one morning before the psychology oral, one of the sisters in my dorm gave me one of her amphetamines. After that, whenever I needed a boost, I'd sneak into the sisters' rooms on my floor and search through their bureau drawers for amphetamines. I took one or two pills from each bottle—there were always enough girls with prescriptions to keep me well-supplied. After class when the sisters came back to their rooms, I used to make up excuses to ask them for a pill, and they always gave them to me. In the beginning, I thought I had everything under control, Father. I knew I was taking too many pills, but I figured I could stop as soon as things slowed down. I breezed through my term papers and orals. . . . I was so exhilarated that I never took time to eat or sleep enough. When I got worried over losing so much sleep, I started taking barbiturates."

Our conversation was interrupted every now and then by phone calls and the admitting of patients. Sister Julia was a very efficient nurse, but her addiction was steadily undermining that. The danger of making a serious mistake —perhaps even a fatal one—became even more acute every day. Sister Julia was called to the admissions office.

When she returned, she suggested that we continue our talk in a quiet corner of the coffeeshop. She resumed her story by telling me:

"After summer school I decided to spend my week's vacation at my parents' beach house—to try to unwind and get away from the pills. But I actually spent most of my time stoned out of my mind on barbiturates, baking in the sun. Mother and Dad complained that I slept too much, but they never suspected why. I kidded myself that I could stop once I got back to the regular schedule of the hospital. How wrong I was. The daily hospital routine I used to love began to tear at my nerves—I snapped at the sisters and had no sympathy for the patients. The slightest excuse was enough to make me take a pill. The other sisters wondered what was wrong, but I always managed to smooth things over until the next flare-up. My supply of pills from summer school was almost gone . . . I was getting desperate! I knew the head nurses kept a strict daily account of all narcotics supplies in a ledger inside the locked cabinet, so I had to dream up a really clever plan for stealing my new supply.

"Whenever I was on duty and it was time to give the patients their pain pills or sleeping pills, I took my keys, opened the cabinet, and prepared the tray of pills—each patient's dosage in a small paper cup. I recorded each dose under the patient's name and distributed the individual cups. Then, contrary to nursing procedure, I left each patient alone—you see, Father, I knew many of them wouldn't take their pills if I wasn't there. Later, when I made the rounds, it was so easy to collect all the unused pills. It wasn't long before I acquired a dangerously high tolerance level for sedatives and tranquilizers. I lay in bed crying night after terrible night—staring into the darkness and—God forgive me—how many times did I pray for death! Suddenly I remembered seeing rows of brown bottles of codeine cough syrup on the shelf just inside the narcotics cabinet. The next night as I went off duty, I unlocked the door and took a bottle—I drank two large mouthfuls right from the bottle, gagging at the sickening flavor, and relocked the bottle in the cabinet. This 'codeine cocktail' became my nightly ritual. Soon Father, I had managed to steal enough cough syrup to fill two mouthwash bottles, which I could keep in my room without fear of discovery.

"For some time I had had the distinct feeling that the doctors were beginning to stare at me and to suspect me—oh, yes, I could intellectualize and try to laugh it off as a classic case of addict's paranoia—but I couldn't shake it! Soon I began to keep my conversations with the nurses and staff as brief as possible. It was not unusual on a rough shift for me to take fifteen to twenty-five pills—just to get by . . . and follow this with several ounces of codeine syrup to put me to sleep!

"The day I passed the twenty-five pill level six months ago was the day I first considered shooting morphine. Can you imagine how I felt, Father, when one day I was unexpectedly asked to lecture to two hundred student nurses? And after the lecture, to face the night shift? By nine o'clock I was coming apart. That shift I had to dispense about eight shots of morphine, and while preparing a syringe, it occurred to me that I could give this woman half a shot—she'd never know the difference. The other half I could keep for myself and record the whole shot under her name—just a new twist for my old plan.

"After that, Father, it was all so easy. Doctors often prescribe painkilling shots for patients after an operation on an 'if needed' basis. Most post-operative patients are too groggy from the anesthesia to remember asking for shots, but the narcotics ledger and the patients' records must list the morphine shots . . . in case the doctors bother to check.

All I had to do was determine which patient really needed his shot and which took it only because he was paying for it . . . and wanted his money's worth. I gave them their money's worth—a shot of distilled water . . . and stockpiled the morphine for myself.

"You know, Father, I'm luckier than most addicts. I never ran the slightest danger of infection from dirty needles or syringes—like hepatitis, staph, or strep. I had an unlimited supply of disposable syringes—sometimes I could quietly steal them from the supply cart. Other times, if I were alone with a patient when I gave him his shot, I just pocketed the empty disposable syringe. If a doctor or relative were present, I just replaced the plastic guard tip over the needle instead of breaking it and threw it in the trash basket. Later, when I made the rounds, I retrieved them from each room. It was a simple matter to sterilize them with alcohol in my room after-hours."

I sat there listening to her over a cup of cold coffee. I hadn't touched a drop. She closed her eyes and took a deep breath, silent for a couple of seconds. She looked so much like a little girl who has done something naughty. But she wasn't a little girl. She was a woman dedicated to a life of service to the sick—a woman herself plagued and crippled by the sickness of addiction. When she met my eyes again, I said, "It's going to be a tough road back, Sister, but with the grace of God there's no reason why you can't make it."

"I desperately want help, Father; I don't even feel like a human being any more. My arms are so sore I'm beginning to give myself shots in the hip. And I'm starting to get careless. I can't keep up with all the schemes I've got going to get narcotics. I forget. The other night I needed a shot so badly I didn't even bother going upstairs to my room. The narcotics closet has an outside door you can close and lock while you're at the cabinet. When you do this, no one can see you from the nurses' station. I went into the closet, rolled up my sleeve, and tied a rubber tourniquet around my arm. I was so scared of getting caught by the head nurse that I was very clumsy. It seemed like an hour before I could pressurize the morphine ampoule correctly to keep the air bubbles out of the syringe. I had just stuck it into my vein when I thought I heard someone at the door. I fumbled with the plunger and then yanked at the syringe. . . . The needle tore open my vein . . . blood went streaming down my arm. . . . I started to cry. The syringe dropped on the floor as I reached for my handkerchief to press against my arm. I ripped off the tourniquet and pulled my sleeve down. As I turned to open the door, I kicked the syringe under the cabinet. Bending down to retrieve it, I dashed my head against the lowest shelf. When I found it, I jammed it into my pocket. I was caught and there was nothing I would be able to say or do. I turned the key and opened the door—there was no one there. The nurses' station was even empty. I hurriedly mopped up the blood on the floor with a handful of surgical dressings and ran up the firestairs to my room to put on another uniform and patch my arm. Then I rushed back as fast as I could before I was missed. Father, my arm is still a mess. I can't go on like this."

The coffee shop was beginning to get a little crowded so we went back upstairs to the small office. On the elevator she showed me the angry-looking gash on her forearm. When we reached the office, I asked her, "Sister, what made you come to a decision to stop now?" She moved uncomfortably in her chair and said, "I'm very sick physically, Father. I know I'm going to have to get something done about my kidneys. Because of the track marks on my body and the urinalysis test, the chief of staff is going to discover I'm on drugs. I'm severely depressed and I've had many suicidal thoughts the past couple of weeks. Father, with all my sins, I still love God very much. I don't want to commit suicide."

I forced myself to smile and hoped it would reassure us both.

"You still have your whole life ahead of you. This is definitely not the end if you're willing to make a new beginning. Are you ready to go down and talk to your Superior now?" The moment of truth had arrived, and her face went pale. "I'm really scared and ashamed, Father, but I'm so tired."

When we entered the Superior's office, she didn't seem surprised to see us. She knew Sister Julia was having problems, but she didn't know why or what they were. Sister Julia admitted that the Superior had tried to talk to her many times without any success. When the Superior heard just exactly what Sister Julia's problem was, she was as stunned as I had been. But in an instant she came to Sister Julia's side and the two of them began weeping in each other's arms. The Superior was a very motherly woman, and this was the sort of tenderness and understanding Sister Julia needed at this time.

I thought I detected a little more sparkle in Sister Julia's eyes. It was a relief to have it out in the open. All those months of carrying that secret buried in her conscience had turned her completely in on herself. She hadn't looked at the world around her or the people in it for two years. She was part of the human race again, and as sick as she was, it felt good to be alive.

Her addiction had come about accidentally. The chances of success with this type of person in rehabilitation is much greater than with those who are motivated by deep psychological hang-ups. This proved to be true with Sister Julia. She is now leading a happy and fruitful life as a nun teaching in a nursing school in one of her Community's hospitals. Looking back, she can't believe it ever happened. She had no intention of becoming a part of the drug scene. No inclination ever existed. Drugs were just something she had read about in the paper. Her world, just like anybody's, could come crashing down for any number of reasons, but she would never have dreamed that drugs would be one of them. Humbly aware of what can happen, she never fails to let her students in on the agony of drug abuse. She tells it like it is, because she remembers how it was.

Epilogue

Although I have spent, and probably will continue to spend, a great many working hours in New York, I am actually stationed at a beautiful shrine that is known as the Shrine of St. Joseph in Stirling, New Jersey. The shrine itself is in the Township of Passaic, the County of Morris, the Diocese of Paterson, and has a history going back to 1924. In that year, Father Thomas A. Judge, C.M., founder of the Missionary Servants of the Most Holy Trinity, acquired a farm on top of a scenic hill in the Watchung Mountains, overlooking a beautiful valley on one side, and the town of Stirling on the other.

In 1928, a large barn was partly dismantled and the heavy beams became the portico of a rustic shrine chapel. The 115 acres of the Shrine of St. Joseph were beautified over the years and enriched by the additions of expansive lawns, flower gardens, and wooded shrines dedicated to various saints. From that time until now, thousands of visitors have come to the shrine and continue to come in all kinds of weather. The peace, tranquility, and sheer picturesque magnificence are tonics to a harried spirit.

But to my way of thinking, the potentialities at the shrine are even broader in scope and penetrate much more into the needs of our society. As do the other priests and brothers here, I spend hours talking to and counseling people who are troubled in some way. This makes my day a busy one. I have held narcotic seminars here at the shrine, and I intend to hold more. During these seminars the young people have demonstrated a willingness to talk about drugs honestly and openly. They have expressed gratitude that now they have a place to go if they do get uptight, if they do get involved with drugs, or if they just want to talk.

The young people who do come here love it, and they each come for different reasons. When I ask them why they come to the shrine, some will answer, "It's peaceful. I like to get away from the city once in a while." Others will say, "Whenever I feel lonely I come up here. There's always someone to talk to." Once I asked a young couple who had just roared up in a Jaguar. Their reply was, "It's friendly; we feel welcome up here." Another time a young man said to me, "I think a lot clearer when I'm looking out over the beautiful valley. I feel closer to God." Each answer is unique, but in the last analysis they all mean the same thing —for many young people the shrine is an oasis in the middle of a loud and confusing world.

I try to place myself in the position whereby the parents of a young person involved in drugs or the young person himself can contact me initially for help. Then, after talking to the parents or the addict, I can refer him or her to the necessary medical, psychological, or psychiatric help. After that, I often supply what is called supportive therapy for both the parents and the person involved, in conjunction with whoever may be working with the addict or parents.

God has been very good to us at the shrine and has blessed our work abundantly. I say "We" because I don't want to give the impression that I am alone at the shrine. Presently there are fourteen members of our Community living here, five priests and nine brothers. Everyone pitches in to do what he can to keep the shrine running smoothly and to be of service to the people who come here. Most of our visitors come during the spring, summer, and early fall months. On weekends you can see hundreds of people milling around the spacious grounds, kids rolling down the long grassy hills, young couples throwing coins into the wishing well, people standing in obvious reverie before the fishpond watching the fountain throw off thousands of rainbowed droplets, or see a head bowed low in silent prayer in the quiet of the chapel.

Amidst all this you will see the priests and brothers trying to make the people feel at home. They are passing the time of day, listening to a problem, giving a word of advice, laughing at a joke, or inviting someone in for a cup of coffee. All the credit for making the shrine as lovely as it is goes to these zealous and dedicated men and the ones who came before them.

In view of our hopes to attract more people to the shrine in the days to come, a new residence with needed facilities is going to be constructed. This will enable us to be of greater service to those who seek our help. A "hotline" is also in the planning stages; it will give teen-agers an opportunity to call up and talk to someone about their problems, especially drug abuse.

As I come to the end of this book, I feel a great sense of gratitude for having been given the opportunity to write it. I have said things long stirring in my heart. In some cases, I have stated the obvious, and in others the not so obvious. It was all done in a sincere effort to encourage, scold, inspire, warn, educate, caution, and strengthen both parents and young people in regard to drug abuse. The heart of this country is beating fast. In many ways it lies sick and feverish, but no amount of drugs will ever cure the malady. Only the personal giving of self, the free exchange of real love and understanding, a hand extended in friendship and peace, only this will alleviate the agonies of our nation and the world.

Our country has the greatest potential in the world, but it can only be realized if our younger generation is alive and physically and mentally competent to assume the responsibilities of future leadership. Without drug abuse the character of our youth is unsurpassed and the future of our country is secure. With drug abuse we are headed into a chaotic decade that will ravish our nation for generations to come.

A wholesome idea of faith must once more be generated by the family, the churches, and the schools. Faith that people can change, faith that people are basically good, faith that once again the world can be permeated with loveliness, faith that there is a God who loves us and cares about us. Faith of this sort is sustaining. It braces and supports like no drug ever could.

This is the kind of faith that produces genuine rebels—the kind I believe in who struggle to preserve pure ideals and solid principles for the betterment of the innocent, not at the irresponsible expense of their injury or death. No chemical can produce such an individual. Only a steadfast faith in the glories of man and the power of God can raise up such a person. I think I best express myself in the following poem:

What name can we call a rebel
No history has belched before?
Annoyer, subversive, ingrate,
A pest at a festering sore.

Phalanx your banners against him,
Traditions unholy and stained.
Pretend he will tire and vanish
Undone by the people he blamed.

No ruse will deter this physician
From tending a stricken mankind.
His scalpel has flashed across nations
A lance for the ills of each time.

Impulsive to those least affected
Less prudent than wise in his cause,
He roars with an eloquent frenzy,
A statesman resplendent with flaws.

The right or the wrong of his battle
Makes tinder for heated debate,
A fool with a misshapen ego
Or a saviour begotten by fate.

When fraud or betrayal of justice
Infringe on the freedom of man,
No image of God will accept it
And a rebel is found in your land.

We need such rebels with a burning faith for justice and truth; not fools with a flaming desire for junk and oblivion!

ABOUT THE AUTHOR

Father Roland Melody was ordained to the priesthood in 1961 and obtained his S.T.L., Licentiate in Sacred Theology degree, the following year, after which he was stationed in Brooklyn, where he was a preacher at retreats and a spiritual director to the Missionary Cenacle Apostolate, an organization made up of lay people. It was during this time that Father Melody began accompanying members of the New York City Narcotics Squad as they made their dangerous, sometimes grievous rounds, and became very involved with the problem of drug abuse.

Father Melody is presently stationed at the Shrine of St. Joseph in Stirling, New Jersey, as moderator of the Missionary Servant Guilds. Besides this responsibility, Father Melody has become more and more involved in drug use and abuse, working for the establishment of a "hotline" for teen-agers at the Shrine, printing a flyer on drug abuse that is distributed to the surrounding schools, and working to make the Shrine a referral center.